# The Highly Sensitive Handbook

PATRICIA WORBY, PHD

# The Highly Sensitive Handbook

## How Sensory Processing Sensitivity and Emotional Overwhelm Hijack your Health

*How to Thrive by Supporting Your Emotional Needs and Healing Past Trauma*

### PATRICIA WORBY, PHD

*Misfit - Weirdo - Freak - Oddball - Outcast - Outsider*

Cover design by Aniqa Anjaz for Patricia Worby

A catalogue record for this book is available from the British Library.

**ISBN-13: 9798854803625**

Independently Published

Printed by kdp, an Amazon.com Company

# CONTENTS

# FIGURES

## ACKNOWLEDGEMENTS

Thank you to all my clients who input wonderful insights into this book and to my family and friends who helped me be the highly sensitive person I am and accepted me anyhow.

To the wonderful Elaine Wilkins and all the practitioners of The Chrysalis Effect (online Chronic Fatigue Recovery program) who encouraged me to present on this very topic and whose unstinting support allowed me to become an author in the first place. I would also like to thank in particular, my client Catriona McCloud – whose insights into her journey into healing as an HSP have been profound. Such is her amazing way with words I had to paraphrase her on several occasions!

# PREFACE

Despite having written seven books already, I have NEVER covered in depth the subject of sensory processing sensitivity and how and why it affects people to develop symptoms of anxiety, depression and often chronic ill health as we get older.

Because modern medicine refuses to see illness as both mental *and* physical (the mindbody connection) these subjects are rarely considered together. This is something I have tried to address with my series of books on aspects of this dual 'Mindbody' approach.

But this omission is causing a great deal of unnecessary suffering. In particular, the understanding of sensory processing sensitivity (SPS) is in its infancy and so has barely been acknowledged outside of psychology. But this is changing. A series of books and podcasts have sprung up talking to people with this personality trait and it is to this need that this book is addressed.

Most sensitive people have a lifetime of feeling 'wrong' or out of place in this hectic world. Some have even been told they're 'too sensitive' or 'you worry too much'. This both instils shame in the person and a belief that somehow, they are *wrong* rather than simply not fitting the neurotypical majority.

However, my clinical practice, and I suspect most medical practice, is dominated by highly sensitive people who have hit a wall or barrier in their lives. Whether illness or crippling anxiety, they find that they can no longer carry on doing what they have always done.

So, this book is a chance to distill the knowledge I have gleaned from working with hundreds of such people (and those who love them) in an easy-to-understand way to help them feel less 'weird' or alone. I want to explain, in simple terms, that anyone can understand how this trait arises and what it means to be this way. Finally, I aim to help them to know not only *why* they are the way they are but HOW to apply that knowledge to enhance their health and find belonging. This is not easy in a neurotypical world that largely ignores us.

And a short note for readers – I have used British English spellings because, well I am British. Therefore, some of the spellings may seem unusual to readers who are used to American English. I think we each need to value and celebrate our cultural differences and I therefore make no apology for that decision.

INTRODUCTION

# Sensitivity – the Kindling to the Flame

Back in 2015 I wrote a book called, The Scar that Won't Heal about chronic stress and emotional trauma. It seemed to strike a chord with people and has become my bestseller. In that book I detailed the physiology and psychology of chronic fatigue related syndromes and why they occur – the perfect storm of toxicity, emotional stress and nutritional depletion. But one thing I didn't have time to go into in much detail was the predisposition of sensory sensitivity and how it affects even people whose childhoods were relatively normal[i]. And that's unfortunate because it makes up 95% of all my clients and I suspect, most of the people who get CFS/ME and other chronic anxiety states.

At the time I wrote it, although I knew about Sensory Processing Sensitivity (SPS) – I had read Elaine Aron's book on Highly Sensitive People after all - I had not made the link with neurological

---

[i] What I term 'normally dysfunctional'. Every childhood has instances of abandonment, betrayal and humiliation but for a sensitive child these states are so much more likely to induce toxic shame states that dictate the rest of their lives.

diversity. This book aims to rectify that omission and help people who grew up feeling different or 'other' feel more understood.

Sensitivity is not an illness or disease. It is a personality trait and although it is a minority of people (20-30% of the population), it is by no means rare. Chances are you are either a sensitive person yourself or you know someone who is.

How can we tell? Well, apart from some of the obvious signs like sensitivity to smells, noise and light which result from the overwhelm of our filtering systems, we also see certain patterns arising in the diseases we get. Anxiety, pain and fatigue are the common long-term results of this trait *when it is not supported environmentally.*

And by that, I mean we grow up in a world that simply does not see the world the way we do, and thus we learn by increments that we are misfits, and wrong somehow.

How could feeling an outsider trigger disease? Well, it's now well known that most diseases are **biopsychosocial** in nature and that if emotional wellbeing is not supported then physical health will suffer as a result of well-established neurobiological mechanisms which I go into in detail in the pages that follow.

It seems that knowledge in this area of neurodiversity is expanding rapidly due to the explosion of neurodevelopmental disorders like autism and ADHD. There are indeed many crossovers in these conditions with SPS – but with one potentially extraordinary difference. When people with SPS are supported emotionally, they actually do better than their neurotypical peers in all aspects of their lives.

This is something we will delve into too as I feel it is one of the most important factors to appreciate. We have a superpower that we are completely unaware of because our culture is in a toxic mess of shame, intolerance and enforced certainties. We have lost the nuance or grey areas of life, which sensitives understand by instinct. It's time to change our toxic culture instead and get together to introduce our special qualities to the world – they are so needed.

# CHAPTER ONE – UNDERSTANDING SENSORY PROCESSING SENSITIVITY

Did you grow up feeling misunderstood – that the world was simply too much for you sometimes? Surrounded by people who couldn't or wouldn't' understand you or the way you viewed the world? Then you were left feeling like an outsider in your own family or friendship group? Perhaps you were lucky enough to find another sensitive soul to shelter with – either human or animal (sensitives often have great soulful relationships with animals).

Growing up we had a family cat, Tibby who lived with us, and he was loved by everyone. However, there was a neighborhood cat, (Binky - a ginger tom) who was perhaps not so well looked after. He would seek me out whenever I was in the garden on the swing my father made for me. I would hear his little bell tinkling on his collar as he ran over, it was always a delight to see him, and I think he felt the same way. Being an animal, we didn't converse, but I would stroke him, and we often spent hours together in the long summer evenings. He was a true companion til he died.

I did have some good friends and a couple I would call 'best friends' during my school years. When my early childhood 'bestie' went to a different secondary (high) school, I felt bereft for a while but eventually made another good friend. Thankfully that was a lifeline as she was kind and helped to protect me from attack. I was not one of the popular girls and, being a redhead, was often subject to horrible bullying. I survived by being diligent and conscientious, but I always felt 'other'. I just assumed like most sensitives that there was something wrong with *me* and strived to be accepted by being 'nice' and people-pleasing. But that never really worked reliably and in adulthood it led me to some disastrous choices.

Without going into too much detail about my experience here[i] – I just want to show you why I've decided to write a book about a very misunderstood but surprisingly common situation – high sensitivity. As a trauma therapist, I work with people from all walks of life who have come to an understanding that something is in the way of them living fully actualized lives. Almost all of them are

---

[i] You can read more in my first book The Scar that Won't Heal

highly sensitive and I have learnt much from them. So, this book contains both a personal and academic understanding.

## Neurodiversity

We have made huge strides in recent years in our understanding of the brain; how it works at a functional level. Because, for the *first time in history,* we can actually map what's going on inside it with functional MRI scans. So, we can now track in real time what happens when a person thinks certain thoughts or watches certain images for instance. We can see how different people's brains respond differently to the same stimuli. You would think, then, that such **neurodiversity** would be much better understood than it is.

### What is neurodiversity?

Why do I consider this kind of sensitivity to be a neurodiversity and not, say, an aberration? Well, it has to do with its evolutionary advantage.

Let's take the dictionary definition to start with:

a variation in normal human evolution which means some people think differently to others. Neurodiverse conditions include autism, attention deficit hyperactivity disorder (ADHD), dyslexia, dyspraxia, Tourette's syndrome and complex tic disorders*

So first off, we see that despite considering natural variation 'normal', in the dictionary definition (and thus the popular belief) it is aligned with a range of diseases or conditions. This is a problem for those of us with high sensitivity as we don't consider ourselves suffering from any condition. It's just the way we are.

But that could also be said about some of the other neuro-diversities. Many mildly autistic people on the spectrum (what used to be known as Asperger's Syndrome), are often unaware of their condition as they've never been diagnosed. Many grow to adulthood totally undiagnosed, particularly women as it manifests differently from men. And, if asked whether they would swap their situation to be 'normal', say no, they have not only adapted to life the way they perceive it, but they *love* that about themselves as it gives them special qualities. So, where does that leave sensitivity?

## A Trait not a Condition

Why is sensitivity a trait not a condition? Well, firstly, it is present from birth (and even before) unlike autism or ADHD which are considered developmental[i]. In fact, there is strong evidence that it is also present in the womb where the unborn child shows stronger

---

[i] By this we mean it develops after birth, although there is much debate about this.

reactivity to light or noise. The majority of children with this trait are either unaware or not bothered too much by it (certainly not til they reach adolescence when comparison with others becomes much more noticeable and intense).

## SPD and the Stress Link

In this regard, it is therefore not to be confused with **Sensory Processing Disorder** (**SPD**) which can be very debilitating and distressing to the child and their parents. It is likely this is due to traumatic early experiences of that child which change the way their brains process sensory information from the senses. Birth trauma (being suctioned or brought into the world by forceps, early forced separation (e.g., ICU) are highly implicated).

Or it can be as a result of stress present in the mother during the pregnancy as a recent study found, "pre- and postnatal stress experiences predicted perceptions of the infant as more negatively and more overall reactive temperamentally"[1] This even has a mechanism of action – stress hormones affect brain development of the foetus. But that is distinct from SPS which seems present in the womb – they are clearly not the same. It's still very unclear, is it a pre-determined trait or a developmental one? That's a very hard question to answer as we will see as it goes to the heart of the nature or nurture debate. We will discuss the genetic variants which seem to influence the development of the trait and lend weight to the nature side of the argument.

## SPS as a Neurodiversity – present in other species

Another piece of evidence to support the fact SPS is a neurodiversity is that it is also present in all other animal species that we have studied (from fruit flies to rats to marmoset monkeys). There is a distinct subset of individuals that have a predisposition to sensitivity from the moment they are conceived. So, it is best thought of as a trait rather than a condition or developmental disorder.

So, if sensitivity is an inborn trait, how did it get to be there? What's the advantage?

# Evolutionary Advantages of Sensitivity

It seems clear that SPS as a trait has developed in all species because it confers some evolutionary advantage to that species. Humans are no different in some ways. We each have a need for shelter/ safety, food, water and loving connection. Perhaps with our abilities to read our environment, sensitive individuals act as 'lookouts' for the tribe. In another more primitive era, we would have been the healers, shamans and artists of our tribe. Called upon to suss out risk – as 'canaries in the coalmine' so to speak. In mediaeval times our extra sensory abilities were called into question, feared and reviled and many sensitives were called 'witches' and persecuted. Luckily our culture no longer fears us so. But since the industrial revolution, we have largely been subsumed into the caring or artistic professions – where we flounder or thrive depending on the support we get. We are a hidden minority, who may not value our extraordinary abilities and even feel embarrassed by them. If you've ever been called 'too sensitive' you'll know what I mean!

## Human Variation

It seems that like most human variation there are genetic and environmental components to the expression (sometimes called a phenotype in biology). I will go into this in more detail later but just to say that genetics are not the sole determinant although they contribute hugely to the predisposition. But there is a strange anomaly, which sets it apart from many other natural variations. It is not evenly spread throughout the population – the 'normal distribution' or bell curve with an average right at the peak – the standard mean' or average of that population.

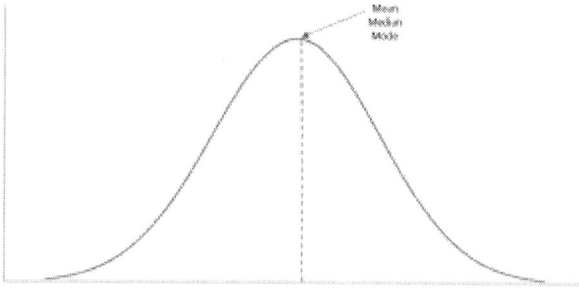

**Figure 1: The Normal Distribution and Standard Mean**

That's not how it looks with sensitivity within the population. We are not evenly distributed at all. Instead, **sensory processing sensitivity (SPS,** as it is properly called) is more like a group of 3 different peaks across the spectrum of the population (a mountain range rather than the mountain). If we plot sensitivity (x axis) to the number of people with that score we would see this:

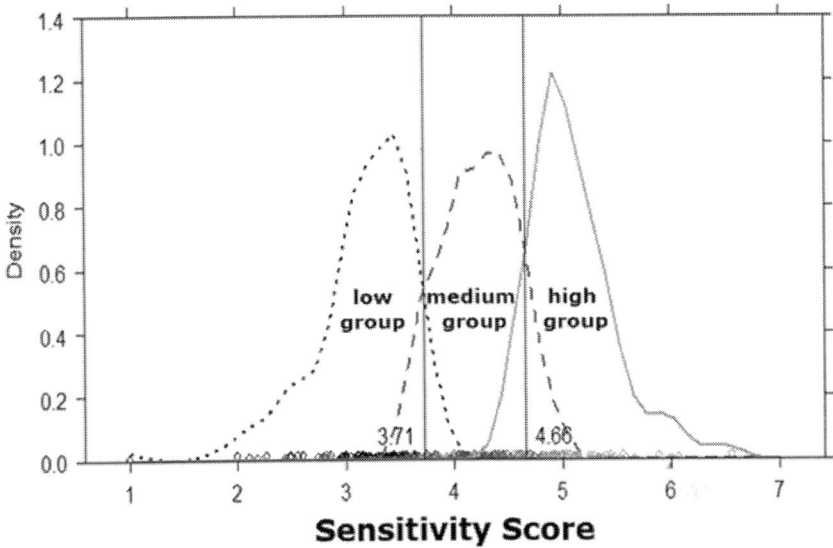

Figure 2: Sensitivity spectrum

We're the high group – the third one on the right. We outstrip the other groups in terms of density but in terms of numbers we're a minority – that 20% - 30% of the population (and in animals) who are the incredibly important as we'll see.

So, who do you know if you're one of that third group - what are the characteristics of being highly sensitive?

# Characteristics of Sensory Processing Sensitivity

It is described quite specifically by the mnemonic DOES which describes the 4 distinct characteristics:

**D**epth of processing

**O**verstimulated/**O**veraroused easily

**E**motionally reactive/**E**mpathy

**S**ensitive to **S**ubtle **S**timuli

**Figure 3: Characteristics of SPS**

See if you can resonate with those four descriptors. Here they are in more detail:

- Depth of processing – we take longer to process information and things are thought about very deeply.
- Overstimulated/aroused – this is very commonly seen in both child and adult HSPs as a need for quiet, non-stimulating environments.
- Emotionally reactive/empathic – this is seen as feeling not only your own feelings deeply but feeling others as well!
- Sensitive to Subtle Stimuli – sounds, smells and textures are perceived by us much more than the average person. Stone in your shoe? Scratchy clothing? You can't ignore it.

If you meet those four criteria, you could reasonably assume you are highly sensitive.

It has 2 components – consisting of heightened:

- Perception of sensory input from the environment such as sound, smell, taste, and touch.

- Cognitive processing of the perceived information about environment, such as thinking deeply about and reflecting on experiences.

So, firstly reality feels different to us but of course we don't know that as we grow up. It's only when we begin to compare with how others see the world (in social contact with others at kindergarten or school). How we see the world is how we perceive reality or the truth of the way things are. We cannot, as humans, exactly know what it feels like to perceive things differently. But eventually we start to see differences in how we react to things compared to other more neurotypical people.

I call it the siren test. For years, if an ambulance or police car passed by with its siren going, I would startle and feel an internal agitation that is hard to describe but 'shakes me up' would come close. Others around me, if asked 'did you hear that?' would say – 'what siren?'

or 'I didn't hear anything'. It simply hasn't made it past their sensory filter (a part of the brain we will look at in the next chapter).

That for me outlines the difference in a nutshell.

How does sensitivity play out for you? Take a minute to read those four points again. If it looks like it describes you, I would highly recommend you do the HSP test. It's free and fairly quick (only 27 questions)[i]. See also my additional questions in Appendix 1.

## Elaine Aron's HSP Study and Questions

A major advance was made by a psychological researcher called Elaine Aron, who, along with her husband Arthur[ii], decided to interview people to find out about differences in reactivity. Her results were first published over 30 years ago in a well-respected but ultimately obscure scientific journal[2]. Her academic colleagues persuaded her to write a book about it and The Highly Sensitive Person resulted. It didn't become an instant classic, but its controversial and astounding results gradually crept into public

---

[i] See Elaine Aron's website **https://highlysensitiveperson.com** for the full list Also see Appendix 1 – my highly sensitive quick questions for some I've developed.
[ii] For once it seems the woman in the partnership has become more famous than the man even though they did the work together. She wrote the book!

awareness. She was asked to give some talks, became better known and wrote a book for highly sensitive children and parents too.

Her research was based on high correlation between certain experiences of her subjects and how they were rated on the sensitivity scale. She wasn't intending to define a new condition or personality style. As she says herself, she:

"Did not 'discover a new trait,' but one that needed a more accurate name than "shyness," "neuroticism," "inhibitedness," or "introversion." Nor was it done in order to write a self-help book—that was not my plan and came later. It all began out of simple curiosity about our use of a common word." (sensitive)

The main impact of her book (apart from to distinguish high sensitivity from the normal range - the other 2 groups were not known then), was to develop a quiz with questions such as:

- I am easily overwhelmed by strong sensory input.
- I seem to be aware of subtleties in my environment.
- Other people's moods affect me.
- I tend to be very sensitive to pain.
- I am easily overwhelmed by things like bright lights, strong smells, coarse fabrics, or sirens close by.
- I have a rich, complex inner life.
- I am made uncomfortable by loud noises.
- I am deeply moved by the arts or music.
- When I was a child, my parents or teachers seemed to see me as sensitive or shy.

There are 27 questions in all which are available on her website[i]. They relate to different sensory experiences of taste, touch, smell and emotional reactivity. It's a really good piece of science because it was *generated from the data* which is how all good science should be. See more details of the study in the box below.

> Research Notes: Elaine Aron interviewed 39 people: 17 men, 22 women. Ages ranged from 18 to 66, with at least 4 in each decade. Although not what we would today consider a large study, it was surprisingly comprehensive: a 2–3-hour interview to ask about their lives, relationships, and childhoods. Elaine made the assumption that introversion was synonymous with sensitivity but 7 of her subjects defined themselves as extroverts according to the Myer's Briggs scale. A surprising number were also securely attached – a measurement related to childhood bonding. The majority though were categorised as 'insecure avoidant on that attachment measurement meaning emotionally you bury your feelings and rely on yourself more than others.

Some of the clients I see have all 27 questions as a yes, but the vast majority score between 17 and 24[ii]. Of course, like all statistical data it's only as good as the questions that are asked. And some are rather specific and possibly gender biased (as the majority of the people she interviewed were women). But as small as the study was

---

[i] **https://hsperson.com/** A good additional question I ask is "if going out do you take your own transport as you want to be able to control when you come home."
[ii] I work with people with chronic anxiety, fatigue or pain, all of which usually correlate to high sensitivity. High is anything over 14 (halfway) in my opinion.

it was incredibly important as it blew wide open the previous assumptions about sensitivity as a *problem* related to shyness or introversion.

## A trait not a disorder

It is important to note we are measuring a *personality trait* here not a disorder. The Sensory Processing SPS designation is a new one which unfortunately may be confused with couple of disorders as outlined in the psychiatrists' 'bible' The Diagnostic and Statistical Manual or DSM (now in its 6th iteration). Elaine is very keen to point out that:

"Sensory Processing Disorder (Sensory Integration Disorder) is not related to what is measured by the HSP Scale or the general construct of Sensory Processing Sensitivity, the concept described here, which is a normal temperament variation found in 20% of the population and, by itself, does not cause impairment or distress.

As a minority state it is often misunderstood by a mainstream world and HSP's often feel out of place, 'wrong' at home, school or workplace. Especially if we are criticized, found wanting or humiliated in front of others. Many people cope with this by using a strategy which makes them appear to be handling things (which may include zoning out or appearing docile/placid) but underneath the mask, the emotions are churning. This is because of the heightened stress reactivity which goes hand in hand with this trait.

As I like to say, "Sensitivity is the gun, environment is the trigger". Whether that be your diet, your toxic exposure or your childhood experience, this is what turns your body's gene expression and physiology into either a building/repair (**anabolic**) state or a breakdown (**catabolic**) (can be positive or negative). So, it affects our long-term health as well as how we feel in the world.

## Comparison with Other Personality Traits

Sensitivity shares remarkable similarities with other common personality traits and can be mapped alongside those measures. Psychologically, personality is usually described and measured across five traits which can range from low to high, these dimensions are also each measured on a spectrum. These are:

- Extraversion (being sociable and outgoing)
- Neuroticism (being easily stressed and anxious)
- Openness to Experiences (being open-minded and imaginative)
- Agreeableness (being kind and cooperative)
- Conscientiousness (being self-disciplined and orderly).

The data isn't conclusive, but studies have shown that highly sensitive people tend to score higher particularly in Neuroticism and Openness to Experiences and lower scores of Extraversion, whilst there aren't so many obvious correlations between sensitivity and Agreeableness or Conscientiousness.

People that had difficult childhoods are more likely to develop high Neuroticism, compared to sensitive people growing up in supportive environments. Neuroticism doesn't sound very positive does it, but it actually just describes the "tendency of sensitive people to be more negatively affected by adverse experiences" which is a common experience for many people particularly in childhood (ACEs). Openness is perhaps the complete opposite and results from a heightened sensitivity to positive aspects of the environment – we feel more uplifted, more aware of our sensory experiences. Lower Extraversion correlation is interesting as it describes sensitive people's tendency to be perhaps a little less outgoing and sociable (more introverted). However, in Elaine Aron's original study about a third of her sample came out as extraverts so it's not mutually exclusive.

As I have described before, development of personality is itself a construct (temperament is more an inbuilt trait) which develops according to people's life experiences. For example, if in your family of origin, you needed to be fun and bubbly to get attention, it's likely this becomes your strategy for life[i]. In contrast if you were rewarded for being serious and academic, that can also become part of your personality. So, in my view, sensitivity is more akin to temperament than personality. It's an inbuilt difference in reactivity of your nervous system. Your personality adaptation may add or detract from that, but it is not something that you change.

It is tempting to try and map sensitivity to these other common personality traits but clearly, they don't explain the full story of how sensitivity expresses itself. There is also the interplay of environment and genetics which we will develop in later chapters.

## Sensitivity and the Stress Response

The stress response shows up in the body regardless of whether it is consciously perceived or not. This is a pathway from brain to body which is designed to prepare us for fight and flight (defence) or rest and digest (relaxation). The balance is ultimately controlled by the messages the body receives from the brain about what it perceives is going on. It is then translated into physiology – the processes of

---

[i] Although this can sometimes not be your authentic self. Children will readily exchange authenticity for attachment (bonding to parents) because the latter is ial for survival.

metabolism, detoxification and repair are affected which shows up in myriad ways as somewhat bewildering symptoms.

This disarray we are left in after such an experience is profoundly disorienting – it may take us hours, days or even weeks to come down from the stress response. Sometimes the effect is lifelong – like an experience of overwhelm when we were very young and unsupported. Alane Freund, who has written a lot on the subject of HSPs, describes being told off by a doctor for wincing when having stitches taken out age 7 when, without her parents there, he started to pick them out with tweezers. She has never forgotten it.

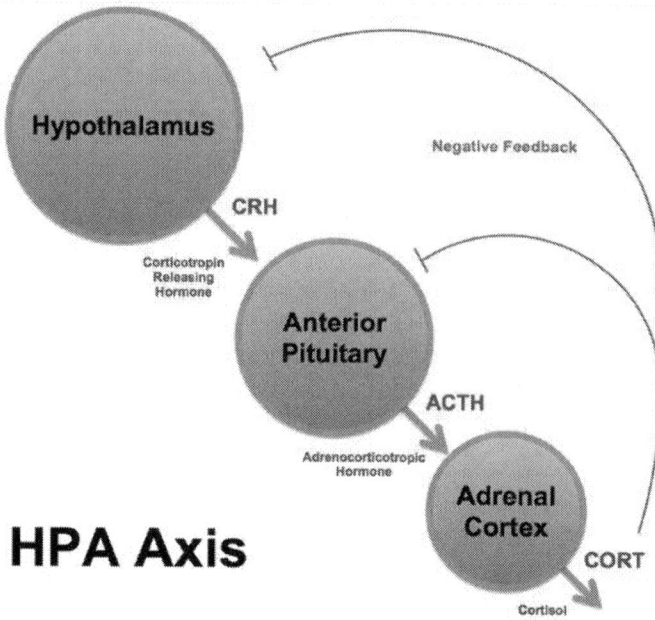

**Figure 4: The Stress Response - 'HPA Axis'**

For me there was an experience when I was a similar age at school and learning handwriting for the very first time (up until this time we had been printing letters). We were practicing joined-up 'o's and I took a short cut which looped them more like a spring which was quicker and I reckoned quite innovative! I proudly presented it to the teacher who proceeded then to loudly exclaim her dissatisfaction by throwing my work into the bin with the immortal words 'this is fit only for the trash!' I was absolutely devastated.  It was so humiliating to be chastised in front of everyone and then sent back to my desk after having retrieved my work.

For a sensitive child this is like being publicly hung out to dry. We can't forget it and go into a state of shock. No child likes being shouted at or humiliated /shamed but for sensitives it cuts like a knife and buries itself in your body for the rest of your life as a belief *about you.*

You may have your own childhood experience that you simply can't forget. Or it may be something that happened to you at work or in a relationship. I have many examples and so do my clients. Many report enduring memories of being bullied or embarrassed, and these experiences live on in their bodies.

For children with traumatic childhoods that is compounded, and their nervous systems never return to rest and digest – they end up in fight and flight pretty much permanently.

## Sensitivity Nature or Nurture?

There is much debate currently as to whether sensitivity is innate or caused by trauma. I certainly think a non-supportive or challenging childhood experience sensitises an already sensitive brain, but I don't think you can say trauma causes something that seems inbuilt from the moment we arrive. You could, I suppose, blame birth trauma but how to explain the foetus? I think it's the old problem in science of 'correlation is not causation'. Which means something like smoking may be correlated with lung cancer but there are smokers who don't get lung cancer so we cannot definitely say it causes it or it would be 10% of smokers.

So, we have a sensitivity which is innate, intrinsic to a person, and does not seem to change much over the course of a lifetime. That is, it doesn't suddenly disappear but may be heightened towards the more easily triggered depending on the environment of that person.

Again, we can argue about nature vs. nurture here but I'll get onto the genetics in detail later. For now, understand it is a predisposition that affects everything about you but most especially predisposes you to fatigue, anxiety and depression in later life IF you have little support for your sensitivity and most especially if you have had experiences which sensitised you further.

Illness as a Sensitiser

There is no more shocking experience than when chronic long-term illness strikes - it creates a downward spiral of anxiety and displacement – who am I if I can't work? Why did this happen to me - I'm so conscientious! How is it that no matter how hard I try I can't get better? The list of negative self-talk of the highly sensitive seeks to compare themselves with their less sensitive peers who seem not to fall ill or recover more quickly. Thus begins the endless rumination which sends us further down the rabbit hole of shame and fear[i].

I can remember as a university student getting some sort of stomach bug (glandular fever maybe?) which resulted in constant vomiting for 3-4 days. No-one could offer me any answer as to why I had this and my housemates (there were 10 of them!) were fine. It felt so unfair, and it left me weakened and shocked. By the time I did recover, I had lost a stone (14ibs) in weight and was barely able to walk without exhaustion. I believe this experience probably set me up for chronic fatigue which descended suddenly at age 34[ii].

## Comparison with other Neurodiverse Conditions

I also wanted just to end with a very basic comparison of SPS and other Neurodiversities, as this is an important topic.

**Table 1 : Comparison with Other Neurodiversities**

---

[i] Neuroscientist Dr Jeffrey Kennedy talks about this in his excellent YouTube podcasts an anxiety and why they originate in an alarm signal in the body.
[ii] Actually, there were precursor issues which I ignored. It felt random.

| SPS | ASD | ADD/ADHD |
|---|---|---|
| Easily overstimulated | √ | √ |
| Empathy/sensitivity to social cues | X | X |
| Withdrawal | √ | X – acting out |
| High sensation seeking (beauty, truth, meaning) | X | √ - |
| Sensitivity to sensory stimulus (sound, light, touch, etc) | √ | √ |
| Present at birth | X | √ |

And just to complete that comparison with perhaps a more accurate representation of how the conditions overlap see the Venn diagram below. Many people have SPS and one or more of these conditions too. My purpose here is not to stigmatise or give a hierarchy of conditions but to illustrate that diagnoses is an art not a science and that SPS sits outside of these neurodiverse conditions. Remember it is an inbuilt trait.

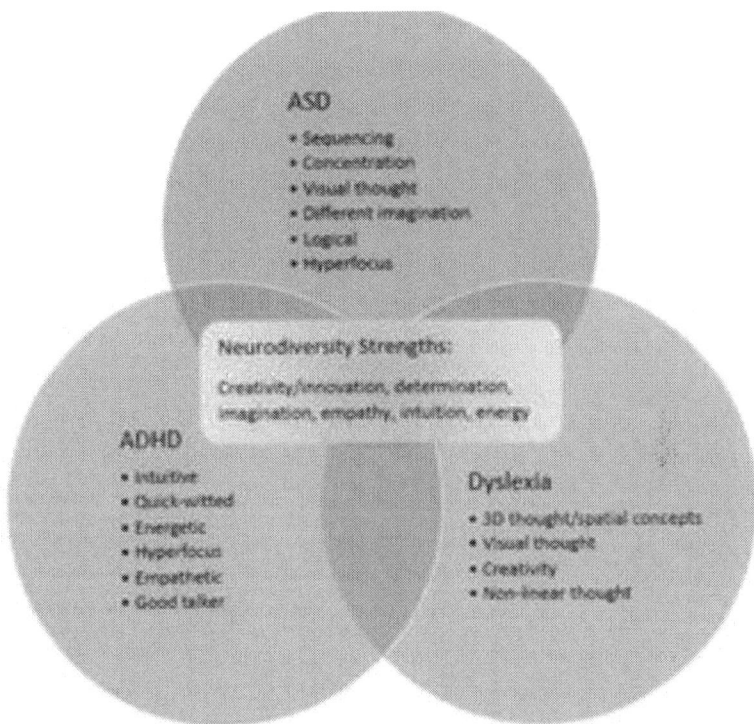

**ASD**
- Sequencing
- Concentration
- Visual thought
- Different imagination
- Logical
- Hyperfocus

**Neurodiversity Strengths:**
Creativity/innovation, determination, imagination, empathy, intuition, energy

**ADHD**
- Intuitive
- Quick-witted
- Energetic
- Hyperfocus
- Empathetic
- Good talker

**Dyslexia**
- 3D thought/spatial concepts
- Visual thought
- Creativity
- Non-linear thought

**Figure 5: Overlap of Common Neurodiverse Conditions**

## Chapter Two – Beginnings: The Highly Sensitive Child

So, we saw in the last chapter that sensitivity is a trait not a condition and that one of the reasons we know this is because it begins in the womb. Let's dive a little deeper into this fact.

## Origins of SPS in the Womb

There have been some studies that show that high sensitivity is present even before birth – in the womb! But it may be that this is due to gestational trauma like being induced or difficulties of the mother in pregnancy.[3] The cause/effect dynamic has not been reliably determined (i.e., is it the chicken or the egg – which shows up first?). According to this recent paper: "few longitudinal predictors are known", which is technical speak for they don't know what predicts this trait long-term. It may be due to epigenetic changes to the stress response system which make that child more reactive[4]. The cortisol response (natures' main stress hormone) is changed for life and may be accentuated, blunted or changed out of its normal rhythm. But whatever the outcome, it's clearly a major effect that changes the life course. It's almost impossible to say which factor is more important, nature or nurture.

But given the new information coming out of the data from adverse childhood experience (ACE) studies (first begun in 1998 by Vincent Felitti, so with a long track record), and the work of such luminaries as Nadine Burke-Harris, we know that the environment that a human child grows up in is the *number one most important determinant of lifelong health and wellbeing*[5]. In the mid to late nineties, it was known that low birthweight was a very strong predictor of many chronic adult diseases including cardiovascular disease[6] - this was called 'in utero or pre-natal programming' by its main proponent, Dr David Barker[i]. There have been some important milestones in this research which began with the work of Thomas Boyce[7] and developed by Michael Ploess[ii], names you will hear a lot of!

---

[i] In whose department at the University of Southampton I was lucky to work, albeit after he had died, but with his team members including Keith Godfrey and
[ii] His website **https://sensitivityresearch.com/** is an extraordinary resource.

# The Orchid vs. Dandelion Child

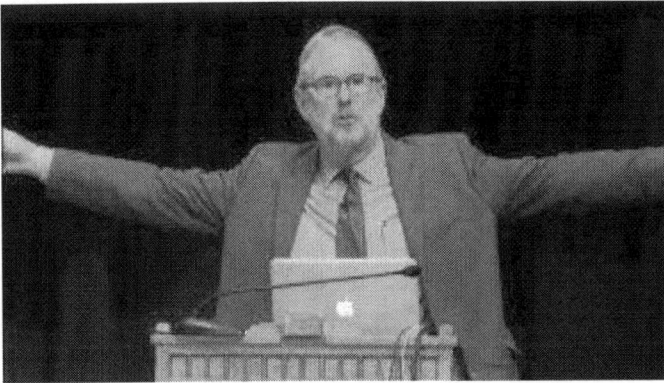

**Figure 6: Thomas Boyce lecturing on Orchid Children**

Tom Boyce is an American researcher who was looking at the variation in sensitivity in children resulting from adverse childhood experiences and he discovered not a gradation across the population but a definite peak of high sensitivity with adverse childhoods that corresponds to the 20-30% of the population with this trait.

This is consistent with what we now know that highly sensitive children are more affected by adverse experiences (and conversely benefit more from supportive interactions) but at the time was at first considered an aberration[i]. However, his research was several years before the SPS research that we see now, so it was not surprising that this was misunderstood. He likened the sensitive children to orchids and those without neurotypical sensitivity dandelions based on the relative ease with which those two plants can establish themselves. Orchids need a much more nurturing environment, or they fail to flourish; dandelions will grow anywhere. It seemed an apt analogy.

His original paper spawned a book 'The Dandelion and the Orchid Child', which I would highly recommend. He also did an illuminating TED talk which outlined succinctly his discovery.

He discovered there were 3 distinct groups of children and those high on the SPS scale (orchids) were much more likely to experience poor health but also success when their sensitivity was properly supported.

---

[i] In fact, Tom and his team thought maybe they had made a mistake as he outlines in his fabulous TED talk.

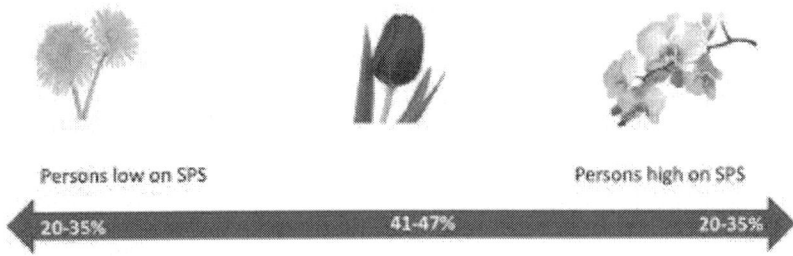

Persons low on SPS                    Persons high on SPS

20-35%                41-47%                20-35%

**Figure 7: Dandelion, Tulip and Orchid Scale**

Subsequent research has confirmed this 3-way structure and that it correlates well with the original HSP sensitivity score, as developed by Elaine Aron. So, it has been corroborated as an accurate measure of sensitivity.[8]

Interestingly, sensitivity becomes apparent to observation in children between the ages of 1-3 in their play so it is clearly not developmental like autism/ADHD which can appear suddenly (and may be linked to toxic assault and failure of brain detoxification or trauma). I talked about this extensively in my books The World Within and

Also, really importantly it can be positive or negative depending on the quality of childhood support – we respond much more to this than neurotypical people. This is called Differential Susceptibility which I will cover later.

Is a real pattern of heightened reactivity not a made-up term to make you feel special. We thus are moving away from the term Highly Sensitive Person and more towards Sensory Processing Sensitivity (SPS) or more simply Environmental Sensitivity.

Furthermore, SPS should be considered a neurobiological personality trait not a condition or disease! This contradicts the medical view that lumps it in with Sensory Processing Disorder (not the same thing at all). Equally looking at it from a psychological point of view, it is not the same as shyness or introversion (a temperament). In fact, there can be sensitive people who are extravert and not at all shy, but they still possess the defining characteristics of SPS.

## Prevalence of SPS

As we've seen, unlike many other human characteristics like height or intelligence it is a spectrum, the 3 peaks of differing sensitivity with the highly sensitive group making up about 20-30% can be mapped over this graph.

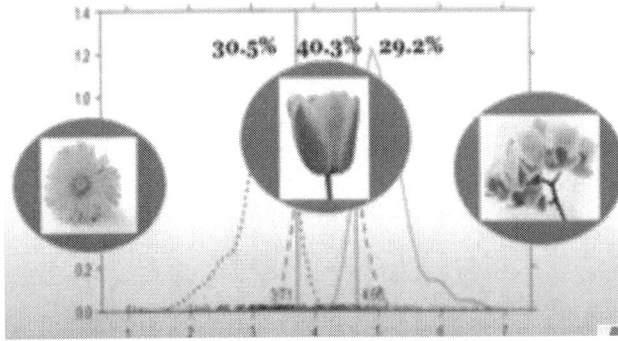

Figure 8: Prevalence of SPS

In the chart you'll see the prevalence: 30% are classed as low, 40% as medium and 30% as high in sensitivity.

## Differential Susceptibility

Differential susceptibility is a clever way of saying highly sensitive people are not only more affected by negative effects of adverse experiences but also *particularly responsive to the positive effects of supportive experiences*. I've been reiterating this to really hammer the point home that it isn't only a negative trait. It just accentuates the importance of a supportive environment.

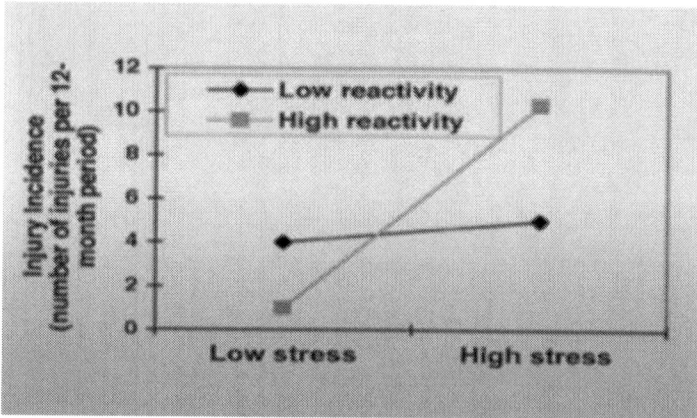

Figure 9: Differential Susceptibility

The interesting thing is a positive childhood environment (low stress) creates *a buffer to negative reactivity* i.e., sensitive children do better in supportive environments than their less sensitive peers in these situations. The theory is supported by empirical studies which are fairly extensive and peer reviewed and has been termed **Environmental Sensitivity Theory.**[i]

This theory states that people differ in ability to perceive and process information about their environment due to neurobiological differences in their brain & genetic differences. It

---

[i] Lionetti et al 2018, Michael Ploess (SensitivityResearch.com) – Queen Mary University & Dr Bianca Acevedo, Neuroscience Research Institute, California

implies this is not something that we can merely *will* out of existence – we can't make it go away!

So, to summarise, because of the heightened physiological stress reactivity (stress response), highly sensitive people show increased sensitivity to both negative and positive experiences. This manifests from your earliest moments and thus has a very important effect on your brain development and nervous system as we will see in the next Chapter.

# CHAPTER THREE – BIOLOGY OF A HIGHLY SENSITIVE NERVOUS SYSTEM

So, now you may suspect you are highly sensitive, and it has always been so. What does that mean in terms of the neurological impacts?

We know that the brains of human beings are tremendously affected by their environment, particularly when young (as humans are born with immature brains compared to other mammals)[i]. Why is this? We have large, complex brains (much larger for our size than other mammals) so in order to get the cranium (the bony surround) out through the birth canal, it has to do a large part of its development *outside* the womb.

Human beings are relational creatures, dependent on nurturing and support in our early years. If our environment is not so emotionally supportive however, our brain development is shifted towards threat perception and the stress response being

---

[i] This is to allow our huge cranium to come through the birth canal.

hyperactive. Let's look in detail at what happens to the brains of sensitive people who grow up in non-supportive or abusive environments (aka who experience adverse childhoods or trauma).

## Neurological Brain Changes

The brain is not fixed or static, it is an ever-changing organ that responds to its environment. It constantly makes new connections between neurons (nerve cells) and sometimes new nerve cells themselves. This is termed neuroplasticity and a way in which the brain can adapt to different circumstances to enhance survival of the organism.

If the environment is favourable, the brain can adapt to safety and creative behaviours: suckling and playing (when young), singing, dancing, laughing and other pro-social behaviours. It learns to anticipate reward from these pleasurable interactions with self and others. Those neural connections are strengthened. If the environment is not so reliable or is downright dangerous (where unpredictability reigns), the brain adapts to anticipating threat and upregulates the fear centres of the brain (amygdala and associated areas of the limbic (emotional) brain). With the secretion of various growth factors,[i] the brain grows more neurons in these regions and slows others that are less needed. This sets in motion a stress response in the body via the connections of the autonomic nervous system which begins at the hypothalamus, down to the pituitary sending messages down the spinal cord.

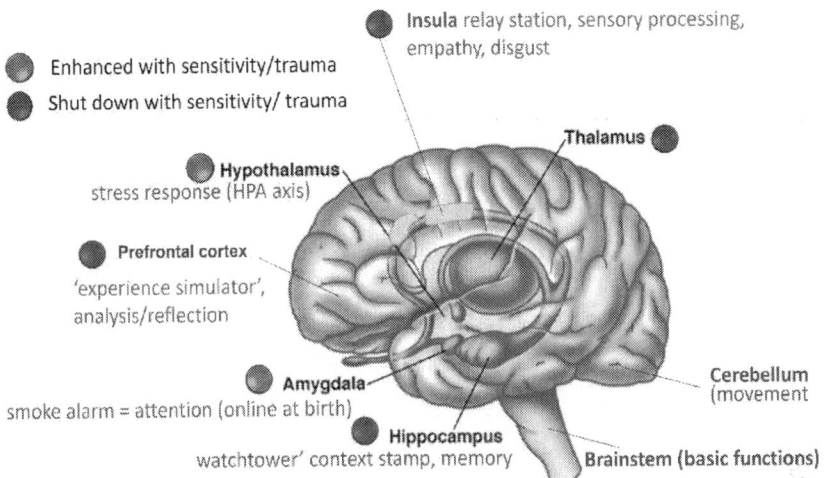

Insula relay station, sensory processing, empathy, disgust

Enhanced with sensitivity/trauma

Shut down with sensitivity/ trauma

Thalamus

**Hypothalamus**
stress response (HPA axis)

**Prefrontal cortex**
'experience simulator',
analysis/reflection

**Amygdala**
smoke alarm = attention (online at birth)

**Hippocampus**
watchtower' context stamp, memory

Cerebellum
(movement

Brainstem (basic functions)

**Figure 10: The Limbic System**

Areas of the brain that grow (increase neural connection):

- **Amygdala**- fire alarm /smoke detector (& procedural/body memory).

---

[i] like BDNF (Brain-Derived Neurotrophic Factor) – a peptide that promotes neurons to grow and strengthen – sometimes dubbed 'Miracle Grow for the brain'.

- **VTA** - reward centre, the dopaminergic response – basis of addictions.
- **Hypothalamus** - threat evaluator (is it safe?). Always on the lookout for danger – hypervigilance.
- **Prefrontal cortex** – experience simulator (analysis of actions – can make us ruminate and over-analyse).

Those areas that decrease in size or connectivity:

- **Thalamus** - relay station (data sifting from all the senses). Can't determine what's relevant or not.
- **Hippocampus** - date stamp and normal memory processing -lose context and ability to process experiences without memory loss or distortion.

Remember these adaptations are a survival response and therefore are prioritised by the brain and body as a means to protect the basic functions needed for ultimate survival. We find that joy and social connection may be sacrificed in these circumstances[i].

This should be a temporary response to a temporary situation but sadly for many children and adults, stress is unremitting because the brain has adapted to a permanent state of stress. A child with a

---

[i] One social interaction that is enhanced and that is the fawn response – one of the few options open to powerless people and children is people-pleasing behaviours that *sacrifice their emotional needs to those of a person in power over them.* These behaviours may continue into adulthood regardless of need because they have become a habit.

highly sensitive nervous system already is at a disadvantage, if stressed as their system already reacts more acutely as we have seen. Add to this ongoing stress and we can guess that the health of that child and their ultimate wellbeing is going to suffer, and this is indeed what happens as we will see in the next chapter.

## Genetic Differences

What about genetic variability? Isn't it all just down to the potluck of which genes you get? Well yes and no. Certainly genetics are an important factor which you cannot change. It turns out that about 40-50% of the differences in sensitivity between people is due to genetic factors, whereas the remaining 50% is environmental. Genes are important but not solely responsible for how you are.

But they're often over-emphasised – mainstream media love to tout the idea that genes are 'good' or 'bad' and what you inherit determines your fate. We call this **genetic determinism**[i] but is no more true than 'karma' or 'god's will' as an absolute determining factor.

---

[i] For instance, the scare over inheriting the BRA-C1 gene for breast cancer. But this is only part of the story and to remove a breast prophylactically is like taking the oil lamp out a car and saying the engine is fixed. You need to change the environment, not remove the vulnerable organ (unless it already has cancer).

For a start there is no one 'sensitivity gene' that automatically creates sensitivity - it is more a combination of overall genetic sensitivity score. Like the rows of fruit in a slot machine – if you get all lemons, then life is going to pretty much suck (excuse the pun).

This is true of many areas of the body, not just the nervous system. I discuss this more widely in the book The Scar that won't Heal using liver enzyme genes as an example.

## Genes Involved in Sensitivity

There are some genes that stand out in promoting a *predisposition* to sensitivity – for the full geeky detail check out this:

**SLC6A4** (solute carrier family 6 member 4) - encodes the serotonin transporter, which plays a role in the regulation of serotonin levels (your happy neurotransmitter). Variations in this gene are implicated in high sensitivity to stress, specifically the serotonin transporter gene (5-HTTLPR – HTP is the precursor of an amino acid called Tryptophan which is involved in the biosynthesis of serotonin). These have been studied in relation to stress resilience and vulnerability. The short allele variant of 5-HTTLPR has been associated with increased stress reactivity and an elevated risk for developing stress-related disorders.

**CRH** (corticotropin-releasing hormone): The CRH gene encodes a hormone involved in initiating the body's stress response. Variations in this gene have been linked to an increased susceptibility to stress-related disorders and alterations in stress reactivity.

**NR3C1** (nuclear receptor subfamily 3 group C member 1): This gene codes for the glucocorticoid receptor, which is responsible for binding stress hormones like cortisol. Variations in the NR3C1 gene have been associated with altered stress reactivity, including heightened sensitivity to stressors.

Genes are Not Your Destiny

But genes are not your destiny – just a predisposition. So, what controls what turns the genes on and off? The answer is perhaps surprising – environmental signals like toxicity, nutritional status and – the big one – emotional state. If you are full of fear, anger, shame or guilt it's likely that your neurochemical signalling will be guided towards the stress response. When that continues unabated, the body loses its ability to rest and repair properly and illness usually ensues. But there are always warning signs that predate a full-blown condition. Here is a short list:

Warning Signs of Nervous System Dysregulation

- Susceptibility to colds and other low-grade viruses.
- Constant infections – tonsillitis, ear, bladder, skin, etc.
- Allergies or intolerances – asthma, eczema, etc.
- Gut issues (driven by gut dysbiosis) – e.g., symptoms of diarrhoea and or constipation (can become IBS or Crohn's).
- Vision problems (the eyes are very susceptible to stress).
- Travel sickness, vertigo (dizziness - sure sign the autonomic nervous system is imbalanced).
- Heart palpitations.
- For women – painful periods/ dysmenorrhea.
- Difficulties tolerating change/ uncertainty.
- Unresolved (generalized) anxiety i.e., not about identifiable issues.

- Excessive focus on control – needing to fix things, achieve, always be perfect, etc.
- Cravings/ addictions.

This list is of course not exhaustive and is only a quick and dirty guide to the most common symptoms I see in people who are in a fight and flight (stress) response virtually all the time – but they may not realise (it has become normalized). Sadly, that is a common experience for many people – author Pete Walker calls it emotional emaciation, which I find a beautiful if sad description of what has become endemic in our culture of ever-rushing/ chasing a result that ever eludes us.

At the base of these symptoms (the body's cries for help) are unresolved/ undigested emotions. If we grew up in a toxic environment, or where our parents did not or could not allow us to express ourselves emotionally, it becomes a habit for us to repress them. And that has huge physiological consequences as the emotions just go into the body (stored in our emotional brain).

## Emotional Regulation

The result of being in fight and flight all the time when we don't know we are (because it's become normal for us) is that our body is always preparing for threat and loses a sense of how to calm and soothe itself. This is the skill of emotional regulation.

And since emotions are linked to the same part of the brain as our autonomic (autopilot) system that controls our heart rate, immune system, hormones and digestion, we are bound to experience symptoms. Not only that but buried emotions will have to find a way out – much like a boiling pot on the stove needs to let steam escape. If they are not allowed to be vented, they will bury themselves in the body as pain (usually buried anger/rage), fatigue (fear) or various other unexplained symptoms.

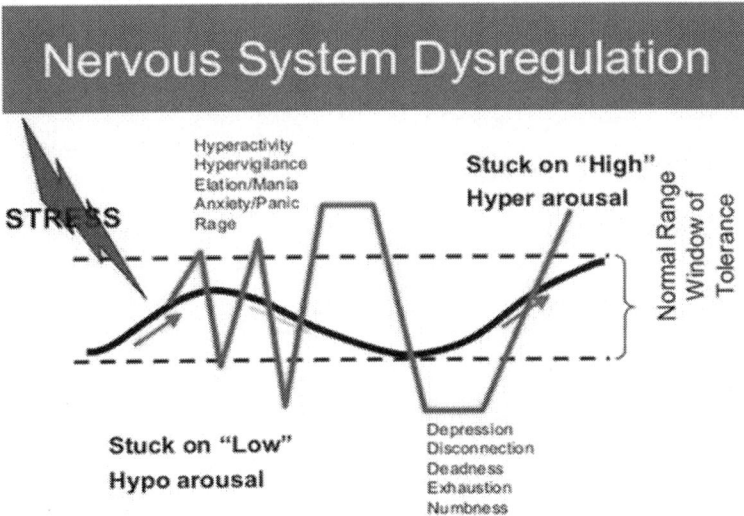

Figure 11: The Nervous System and Stress

So, physical symptoms become the way the body speaks to us. Scientifically this is explained because the part of the brain that deals with pain (the thalamus in the limbic system), does not distinguish between physical and emotional pain and so the wires can get quite crossed. But more holistically I see the body as communicating its pain in the only way it can.

## Illness as a Trigger for Dysregulation

What if you are highly sensitive and you do get ill? You find the symptoms becoming more and more troubling, or they start to affect day to day functioning. Most people head to the doctors in order to get a diagnosis of what's wrong with them and these days that will involve testing rather than the signs and symptoms that doctors used to rely on. Doctors are seldom highly sensitive people – those that are, usually don't make it through medical school (which is in itself a traumatic training which relies on competition and sometimes even shame to motivate people).

It is interesting that sensitive people make up the vast majority of patient appointments at GP surgeries. Why would that be? Largely for two reasons:

- They notice changes in their own bodies quicker than most people as they are sensitive to sensations.
- They are more likely to worry about what it means and jump to the conclusion that it is something truly dangerous.

They may spend a long time waiting for test results to give them an answer as to why they feel the way they do. This adds to the stress of waiting for a definitive diagnosis. But medicine over-relies on testing now to the detriment of signs and symptoms being assessed in person by a skilled doctor who is looking at and touching you to assess what's wrong. This means that although the results are probably going to find serious illness much quicker, for long-term chronic low-grade conditions, it's unlikely to find anything wrong. People then get labelled as medically unexplained and begin to doubt their own sanity.

## The Value of a Diagnosis

What is the value of a diagnosis? It's important to understand that medical science is largely educated guesswork when it comes to chronic (long-term) conditions for which there is no out and out cause. For instance, chronic fatigue is a diagnosis made by ruling out all other organic causes (a diagnosis of exclusion). Diagnosis therefore is a comparative task and because there are many overlaps in clinical conditions (particularly in mental health), your diagnosis may not be the panacea you initially believe it to be.

Labels are helpful sometimes to give people an explanation for why they feel the way they do but don't expect that to lead to a solution! This is particularly true of chronic pain and fatigue, which often has repressed emotions as its base. Look at the diagram which shows that pain and emotions are dealt with in similar parts of the brain. The processing of emotions is meant to happen spontaneously as it does in animals and be supported by others. But in many families, this doesn't happen, or the child is ridiculed or shamed for feeling emotions. Here then the buried emotion is processed as pain – the nerve pathways are very interlinked.

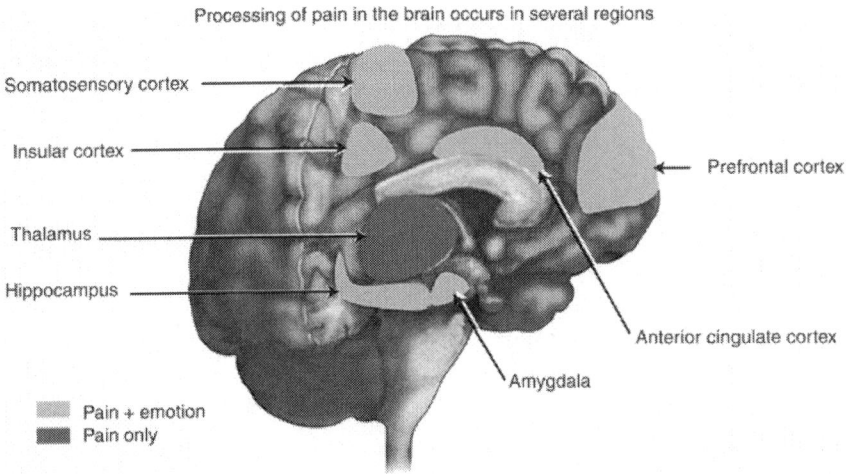

Processing of pain in the brain occurs in several regions

Somatosensory cortex

Insular cortex

Thalamus

Hippocampus

Prefrontal cortex

Anterior cingulate cortex

Amygdala

Pain + emotion
Pain only

**Figure 12: Pain and Emotional Brain Processing**

## Health Sector Interaction Considerations

Within the health sector we need to have a radically different relationship with our healthcare providers. Being told /dictated to as many do is not sufficient. It instils fear. We need to be able to advocate for ourselves and work in partnership with our healthcare practitioners. We need to be able to ask the questions we so need to hear and have input to be able to change our treatments, so we are consulted more and dictated to less. Of course, this is also very challenging in the current health climate where resources are tight but if you are able to ask your doctor or clinician to be aware of their language this may radically change the outcome to one that is more positive[i].

It is interesting to note that sensitive children and adults occupy most GP appointments as they notice their symptoms more and are more likely to be anxious about them!! So, it's a double whammy where we are both more likely to need support but less likely to get those needs fulfilled.

## Gender Differences

Are women more sensitive than men?

Interestingly, no! Studies have shown that 50% of highly sensitives are men but they often don't self-report due to cultural bias (men are not supposed to be sensitive but bury their feelings – stiff upper lip and so on).

Sensitivity is culturally considered more of a feminine trait and therefore more likely to be accepted and expressed by women and girls. However, there is a caveat – we need to take account of the key role of socialisation where girls are expected to model

---

[i] As an example of what NOT to do – I was told just before a routine colonoscopy 'this is where we really hurt you!'. A joke by the nurse of course, but not funny at all and caused me to have a very severe reaction to the procedure.

themselves on others and minimise their own needs. Not only does this teach females to bury their emotions but it often this masks the issue of what is going on under the surface when to all intents and purposes they seem to be doing ok, like the image of the swan on water where the top glides along and the feet are busy beneath the surface. This is similar to what we are finding with autism now... girls tend to mask much more successfully and are able to model 'normal' behaviour for a while til it becomes unsustainable.

For men, they often reach breaking point when they suddenly become responsible for someone else's happiness[i] i.e., in a relationship or having become a parent for the first time. Sometimes the responsibility is unbearable, or they may have so much embedded shame[ii] that they doubt themselves (of course this occurs to women too). It's called 'imposter syndrome' and is most commonly talked about in relation to women at work, but it applies to men too, especially in situations where they feel less secure than they believe they ought to.

---

[i] Although in truth no-one is truly responsible for another's happiness, we often bear the burden, and men, in particular, may feel the need to provide security when they don't feel secure themselves.

[ii] Shame is not necessarily feeling ashamed of oneself but is a feeling of not being enough or wrong somehow, or even 'an outsider looking in'.

Both sexes may feel overwhelmed juggling work and family needs but for men that may express as a lessening of sexual performance and for women a reduction in desire (which requires a blend of autonomic sympathetic and parasympathetic stimulation).

## Impact of Hormones

Men and women are very different in their neurobiological physiology – and never more obviously in the way that hormones affect functioning.

In men there is a steady drip feed of testosterone to the hypothalamus, in women the balance of oestrogen and progesterone cause cyclical variations in emotionality and energy.

### Menstrual cycle

PMS is a very common experience of many women which affects cognitive functioning and emotionality. They can feel extremely on edge, angry or tearful in the run up to a period. As a highly sensitive woman, you are especially vulnerable to the changes and may over-interpret your body's signals with a stress response. Migraines are incredibly common around this time. Modern medicine can't really explain migraines, other than a biophysical sensitivity of the vessels leading to the head. Because it doesn't look at the totality of the human experience, it has nothing to say on the subtle ingrained misogyny or shame that many women feel about their femaleness.

This may come out at puberty when it becomes impossible to ignore the changes that they are experiencing in their bodies which may imply weakness or inferiority in the subconscious mind. This can then get ingrained as a rejection of their identity as a female, certainly we are seeing an epidemic of gender dysmorphia, primarily in pubescent females[i]. Women are taught to hate and fear their bodies as maleness is considered easier and less troublesome. I believe body shame underpins conditions like endometriosis (where uterine tissue grows outside the uterus).

The misogyny that underpins this is so insidious that it is almost unremarked. Women's cycles are seen as an inconvenience at best and a curse at worst, and nobody teaches women to celebrate the changing moods and sees the links with moon cycles. If we had a culture that celebrated women as the backbone of the family and celebrated our strengths, girls would not suffer such debilitating stress around puberty and then later on at menopause.

---

[i] I will cover this in my next book in this series Misfit – Celebrating Being Different

Menopause

Any issues a woman may have had with puberty are usually revisited at menopause. Now the issue isn't the suddenness of menstruation, but the ending of a part of her life (fertility) which may feel like a loss of identity, if there is no support for the benefits of wisdom and freedom which menopause should bring. For many women it is a time of great turmoil and suffering. Quite apart from the hormonal impacts of loss of oestrogen (which can give horrible symptoms), there is a lifetime of toxic load to deal with biochemically. It is treated by our culture as an illness with HRT as the inevitable cure, but in reality, it's just a passage through a portal of change. When the adrenals take over from the ovaries, there can be an exacerbation of stress symptoms for highly sensitive people who already feel stress more acutely.

Getting support and acknowledging that you're suffering are vital approaches as well as detoxing and supporting the body biochemically with herbs and supplements. We must acknowledge what we've maybe repressed about this time in our lives – are we fearful, do we feel suddenly bereft (especially if we've wanted children and couldn't have them?). It is an ending of one phase that can be particularly hard on SPS people (we don't like endings!).

Allowing the guidance and wisdom of older women who have already gone through this phase of their lives, is vital. These voices are largely absent from mainstream culture, indeed older women are generally invisible.[i]

## Andropause and the Male Experience

It's not often acknowledged that men go through subtle shifts at middle age too. A change in the levels of testosterone can induce feelings of lack of vitality. And mentally/emotionally they may struggle to feel manly when the body is shifting into middle age. As a sensitive man, you have likely never acknowledged this, at least not comfortably, without self-denigration. The culture must change to accept male sensibility as it is so needed and helps to balance the somewhat crazy focus on achievement and mindless consumption that plagues our culture. There also be problems with penile dysfunction (another horrible medical term), which affects many middle-aged men and causes great shame. It is such a badge of pride in our culture that when it becomes more difficult to sustain an erection, men suffer great shame. If more men realised it could be an early sign of cardiovascular disease rather than something

---

[i] It is still the case sadly that older women routinely lose their jobs for being too old in industries such as TV/media and hospitality (airlines for example).

unknown or random, more could be done. However, we cannot ignore the extra stress that sensitive men suffer from being supposed to be always strong and the pressure to perform which weighs heavily on them.

## It's the Environment, Stupid

For both men and women, it is vital to know it's not you that is at fault, it is the environment that no longer serves you and that must change. Whilst you may feel it beyond you to change mainstream culture, you do have the power to accept yourself and create an environment where you can thrive. This may be about changing jobs to one where you have less stress or downsizing your house to reduce your financial burden. You may need to address your childhood issues that you have masked with over-work or achievement goals (busy-ness). Do whatever needs to be done, to take off the burden of responsibility - it will have huge benefits for you and those that love you. It's not to say you have to give up on life, you just have to refine it to suit you. More on that later.

In the next chapter we are going to look at how stress is not just the obvious external stresses or work, money worries or relationships, it is also the accumulated burden of unprocessed emotions from early life experience. This is the elephant in the room for most people, even if they had a perfectly 'normal' childhood. And it is doubly difficult for HSPs who may not have been taught how to process their emotions safely.

## CHAPTER FOUR – CHILDHOOD SENSITIVITY AND ADVERSE EXPERIENCE

We have seen that high sensitivity is present from birth and that it can be observed in the play of young children. But how does it manifest in ways that an attuned parent can pick up and what can be done to help the child navigate this process?

## Highly Sensitive Children – Issues

Highly sensitive children are different – there's no escaping it. They may express this as finding it difficult to eat new foods (or foods with certain textures or colours). They may complain of being distressed by scratchy clothing and insist the labels are cut out or that only certain styles or fabrics are worn. They may have difficulty sleeping as their minds are too active and the emotions churned up at night. Sadly, they may also experience bullying or humiliation at school for their reactivity, which is obvious to other children (who can be exceedingly cruel at punishing this).

Just understand these children are going to need a lot more support and less punishment than an averagely sensitive child. The naughty corner does not always help with behaviour because it is not driven by willful processes (i.e., cognitive). The needs of highly sensitive children are much more about supporting them to understand their emotions and help them be processed. Someone who can sit with the child and explain that their emotions are important and understandable can go a long way to calm the anxiety that sensitive children often feel when they are out of sync with the majority. As an example, witnessing the pain or suffering of another (particularly animals) is something the child may struggle to deal with. Giving them practical ways in which they can process their grief or empathy is key. Empathy may indeed be a double-edged sword – the child may feel others' pain so will want to reach out to soothe and help but often to the detriment of their own needs for soothing. A good example occurred to me age 4 when on the first day of pre-school, holding the hand of a girl who was crying and being told that she just needed to grow up and not to encourage her! Or one of my clients who, experimenting with role play and being told it's silly or inappropriate for their age or gender, etc. These messages are never forgotten and instill an incredible amount of shame.

Schools that focus on punishment as a means of enforcing discipline are not going to be helpful for this kind of sensory processing, so making sure you child is in the right environment as much as you can, and having someone to advocate for them in that environment (which may end up being you, but if there is someone in the school who has some understanding of this trait, then that will be helpful to get them on your side).

Supporting their emotional development as much as their educational learning is essential but sadly devalued in most state schools, already struggling on limited budgets. But remember you as a parent can do much to mitigate. Provided you received that kind of nurturing parenting yourself, it is something you know how to do naturally. Of course, that is something many of us did not have. And that is one of the reasons that trauma is transmitted down the generations. The other being that the way your genes switch on and off (epigenetics) is also transmitted. So, if your parents had any sort of trauma in their childhoods, it often sets up a predisposition to stress in the offspring. This has been reported in up to 3 generations in humans (and up to 7 in rats!!).

## Childhood Trauma and Adverse Childhood

# Experience

Sensitivity is the gun and environment pulls the trigger - but what sort of environment makes the most lasting impression? It is perhaps adverse experience that affects your nervous system more lastingly how to react. We would hope that we learn from joyful and supportive experiences but the **negative bias[i]** of the brain suggests that it is *challenging* experiences that most train our nervous system the most[ii].

## Trauma: A Definition

Let's remind ourselves what trauma is: it is not only what is currently understood as trauma – physical or sexual abuse. It can be *anything that overwhelms a child's capacity to cope*, and, as we have seen, that is much more likely in the sensitive child.

This could be that a child had a difficult birth (e.g., forceps or Ventouse, or emergency caesarian), where the mother and child were both stressed during the birth. It could be the child was premature or suffered a chronic condition that entailed

---

[i] Our limbic brain is more likely to react to uncertainty as threat.

[ii] Although we have seen in Chapter 2 that a supportive environment will elevate the sensitive child more than its non-sensitive peers, it is negative experiences that differentiate us the most in adult life.

hospitalization (jaundice is common), or even that they failed to latch on when nursing and were bottle fed! Little things make a big difference to sensitive children and a failure to bond early on is a very big determining factor for your stress response and therefore life experience.

Thus, this broadened definition of an adverse childhood is experienced by much larger numbers of people. It is often the accumulation of small things that did not go quite right for the child and not always one filled with great suffering[i].

Whatever the cause and however it manifests, the traumatized adult is at much greater risk of developing anxiety and depression, and especially so if highly sensitive if they experienced adverse circumstances (especially in childhood). This is especially marked in women. See Figure 13.

---

[i] The ACE score of 10 questions is one that focusses on traditional traumas of abuse and violence or abandonment. See **acestoohigh.com**. The expanded ACE score focusses more on the broader definition and is available online at the CDC.

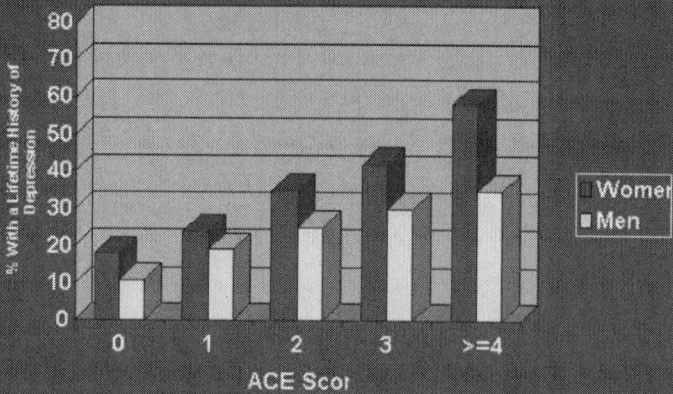

**Figure 13: Childhood Experiences Underlie Depression**

It also has extremely high correlation to addictions like alcoholism and smoking, lifetime experience of suicidality and physical health issues such as heart disease and cancer. This remarkable information is still relatively unknown in medical circles, despite the overwhelming evidence[i].

Doctors are not trained in psychological factors let alone trauma. And they don't have time to ask their patients what happened to

---

[i] One doctor trying to change this is Dr Nadine Burke Harris. See her talk **here**.

them. There simply isn't time in most primary care appointments which are focused on symptomology and the quickest solution.

Trauma release work is available privately (free treatment is possible for those on low incomes but waiting lists are huge) and is mainly focused on interventions such as EMDR[i] or talk therapies.

So trauma is any experience which you weren't able to process at the time, which gets stored in the body as a series of beliefs and rigid behaviours that then reinforce the belief. A parent or grandparent suddenly dies and the adults rarely if ever talk about that person again. The child feels somehow, they must have *caused* the death if nobody even mentions them! It must be their fault (this is termed magical thinking and is common in childhood).

Indeed, it is more often than not the things that weren't present that needed to be present that traumatize the child. If you were the black sheep of the family in some way, or were too much for a parent, or had to take too much responsibility too young, these are ways in

---

[i] Eye movement and De-sensitisation and Reprocessing. Using eye movements to stimulate memory processing to a state of the memory being over and done. Sadly, most people's traumatic memories are stuck in the ever-present now. See my book The Scar that Won't Heal for more information on this.

which you learn that you are alone and unsupported. And that is the trauma which keeps it going.

Trauma is effectively then unresolved emotional memory of bad things that happened or good things that didn't happen in your earliest life experiences which shape the brain to focus on threat more than safety. And 'small-t' trauma as it is termed, is extremely common.

## Trauma, Family Dysfunction and High Sensitivity

Dysfunctional families are now so commonplace as to have become normal. Many of us deny the emotional defects or downright soullessness of our upbringing, with denial or idealisation. I saw this clearly when studying for my PhD in the traumatic components of chronic pain. There were 2 groups of people. Those who recognised the abuse or neglect they had suffered (because it was overt- maybe physical, sexual or verbal abuse). But the second group idealized their childhoods. When describing their parents there were terms like 'angels', 'perfect', 'wonderful'. Of course, a good proportion of the population had childhoods that were materially ok, who did not suffer abuse or neglect and were indeed deeply loved. But no parent is perfect, all of us have defects, do the best we can but the reality is that it's hard and many of us are so stressed that we struggle to do the best for our children. So, this began to ring alarm bells in me. Their parents were their best friends, there was an enmeshment that struck me as unhealthy.

I remember being in the audience at a trauma conference (yes there are such things!) with Dr Gabor Mate – one of the most compassionate human beings who treads this earth currently and an expert in this field. He asked for any audience members who didn't have any trauma effects from their childhoods. A few hands went up. To a woman in the front row, he asked if he could investigate her story a little bit. She said she couldn't remember anything but fun in her childhood. She had a great time with her siblings, she remembered, they looked after each other. He probed some more – what were her parents like? Her mother was troubled, an alcoholic, but seriously it hadn't really affected her that badly. Her Dad was largely absent.

She remembered being with her siblings most of the time, they looked after each other, they had loads of fun, she remembered. She did remember her mother often passed out by the evening and they had to cook their own tea. She was 4 or 5 she thought (before cognitive memory comes online). He asked her if she had children of her own. "Yes, two" she said. He asked her to imagine what it would be like if one of her children found her passed out on the floor. She stopped and went quiet for a moment. "They'd be really scared and distressed, I guess". He asked her to think about how a child of that age can understand what's happening with an absent or neglectful parent. They can't. They can't rationalize, they can only react. And how those children dealt with it was to bond together and get out as soon as they could. Selective amnesia for these experiences is very, very common.

Now obviously this is an extreme example. Most childhoods don't have something so overt to look back on. But many do. And highly sensitive children can be affected deeply by very small absences, not just the big ones. Let me give you a more subtle experience from an amalgamation of my clients' experiences. A sensitive child, Lucy is brought up in a middle-class home, with loving parents, but mum is dissatisfied with her lot. She wants to retrain so that she can contribute more to the family income, so she decides to take a teacher training course which involves leaving her children with a childminder (a neighbour) 1 night a week. Lucy's brother Simon gets on just fine (he's not highly sensitive), but Lucy is not.

She won't play, she just disappears into herself (a common sign of a distressed or overwhelmed child), so everyone assumes she's fine and leaves her to it. Years later, Lucy finds herself unaccountably depressed on a Tuesday. She has no idea why. Investigating further we find that this was the day after her mother's course, when she would have had to go back to school and pretend everything was normal. But she didn't feel normal. She felt totally rejected by her mother. They had been everything to each other growing up and then her brother came along and broke the spell a little, and now this total disruption.

It's not at all logical, it's not something you can tell yourself to snap out of. It's an implicit (unconscious) memory of distress, fear, and loss. And it comes up again decades later as a feeling of depression, unaccountable sadness without reason. Memories like this weren't able to be processed at the time because there was no other person around to be with that child in their sensory processing. If mum had been able to be there with the child, cuddle her and tell her it was only for one evening and it was so they could have a better life, maybe Lucy, and children like her, would be able to know it wasn't their fault, they weren't being rejected or abandoned. For, sadly, this is how a child will interpret the little absences, the little things that don't happen that should have happened.

This isn't to say we all have to be perfect parents by the way. Good enough parenting is where you can acknowledge the differences in your children and allow the sensitive ones to have more comfort, more explanation. We just need flexibility of approach and a school system that doesn't stigmatise sensitivity with punishment[i].

## Schools and the Highly Sensitive Child

We also need to consider the wider context of social situations, particularly schools where children spend a large part of their day. Schools are under enormous pressure right now with budget cuts and struggling to recruit teachers so teaching support and pastoral care has diminished hugely. This means that many children are showing signs of extreme anxiety with eating disorders and panic attacks on the rise. Schools where punishment is the norm and behaviour is controlled this way are far more difficult for sensitive children (and hence boarding schools where children have no respite from that culture are especially difficult). Being sent to a

---

[i] For more information on this please see Gabor's excellent book The Myth of Normal and 'The Tao of Fully Feeling' by Pete Walker.

special room to 'calm down' (alone and unsupported) does nothing to alleviate the neurological triggering which needs social support of a calm other. Being forced to stand alone in the playground (as I was once forced to do) only stigmatizes the child and shames them.

Shame as a controlling method is vastly overused. It is a normal part of social development between the ages of 3.5[i] but beyond that, boundaries need to be negotiated rather than enforced. School memories of shaming are ones that many adults never forget, and it shapes their beliefs about themselves. If they were told they'd never amount to anything or that they were 'stupid', this leaves a lasting impression. We need to take sensitivity into account at school with more support and less shaming. Of course, many schools do their best, but just little tweaks can make a big difference. Having time outside with nature, being able to talk to someone (not necessarily an adult but supportive older child

---

[i] When we admonish children at that age not to do something, this shames them, but this can be repaired easily with a cuddle or reassurance that it is for their own safety or wellbeing e.g., don't poke your brother with that stick, that's naughty. Then you distract them with something else or otherwise draw attention away.,

sometimes works[i]) and using art or music to express their emotions are vital.

## Work Environments and the Highly Sensitive

These factors are similar to the considerations needed at work. Work environments are often very challenging: high stress, competing demands and the subtle unspoken relational demands – having to please bosses and compete with others who may not share our values. Finding compatible work environments is one of the first issues many sensitives have to face.

Sadly, the kinds of work we are drawn to (vocational, with a sense of giving something back e.g., HR, teaching, healthcare, social work) are often the most stressful ones where the pressure is relentless. If at all possible, non-sensitive colleagues need to be educated to understand and give sensitives time/ space to process and different work environments with less pressure/ judgement and more support. Although this is seldom possible as the cultures are designed for the neurotypical, if we had the same awareness as

---

[i] Although I had a client who remembered with shame being forced to sit with an older child who was supposed to help but it made it even more strange… so it's very difficult to give hard and fast rules. Ask the child what would help them.

that for people with ADHD, etc it might be possible to adjust certain practices and environments so that sensitives might thrive.

Unfortunately, it is more often the case that sensitives force themselves to fit with devastating consequences. They will push through the ever-burgeoning workload until inevitably, perhaps, they burn out. Then it is usually a case of going on sick leave to recuperate. Some never return as the prospect of returning to work is one that their bodies rebel against. This is when the symptoms that develop get so serious that people end up chronically ill.

## Bullying at Work

Sadly, one thing I see over and over with highly sensitive people is a tendency to experience bullying at work by bosses and supervisors – anyone in authority over you can take advantage of your goodness and pliability. Because HSP's often grew up in situations where their needs weren't met (often with a narcissistic parent), it seems familiar to them to be overburdened and treated badly. So, if we don't establish our boundaries well, we get pushed around.

In my experience this happens over and over until we learn to say no and keep our boundaries very clear.

Let me give you an example – this time from my own life.

# Case Study – Me

When I was 22 and fresh out of university, I went to work in a big teaching hospital in London working on Muscular Dystrophy research (a congenital disease that affects boys causing disability and early death.) You can understand that with a degree in biochemistry and physiology, it should have been the ideal job for me. Helping others! Tick. Moving healthcare research onwards. Tick.

But it didn't work out that way. My boss was a very unpleasant man who thought very highly of himself (I would say now a classic narcissist). He took what seem like an instant dislike of me. Firstly, I was a woman (still not treated equally in science then), and secondly, I wasn't privately educated (he was). I noted that most of his team were from that background and almost entirely male (I didn't make this judgement then but in retrospect). The women resided almost exclusively in one department where they did the clinical assays (testing). This was considered suitable for women as it relied on repetition and detail. I got on great with these women and they became friends outside of work, so I knew it wasn't just me being difficult.

My role as it was described in the job description was to be part of the team and take part in understanding the causes and genetic treatment that would enable us to eradicate this particular disease. It became very apparent my role as they saw it was to clean up and make endless supplies of assay solution. When my boss made a remark about my lateness one day (I was 20 mins late due to traffic congestion), I saw red. Because he never got in before 11 in the morning, I got very angry and let rip (unfortunate!). Then I went to our senior boss and complained. He said – I'd like to help you, but I can't afford to upset him, he brings in all our funding! So, I had to resign which was very tough as it was a dream of mine to be in research. But the situation was clearly untenable, and I probably saved myself a whole load of unnecessary stress.

The Traumatic Professions – Social Care, Law and Medicine

There are some professions that by their very nature are traumatic. And despite that being very hard for highly sensitive people, they are often drawn to them, particularly if it matches their values. Perhaps a member of the family was already involved, or you grew up wanting to make a difference somehow – then medicine, law or social care can attract you.

Medical training by its very nature is competitive and, in some cases, humiliating. If you do survive the training, you may end up burning out early. Law (and by this I included probation and the prison service as well as being a lawyer), works with highly traumatized people and can also be humiliating when facing the judicial system which pits you against others. I have in fact recorded **an interview with a lawyer** who now works to advocate for better mental health awareness in this profession (see Resources at end).

However, there is another way – we can retrain our nervous systems by working in partnership with it and finding alternatives to the jobs we thought we 'should' cope with but couldn't. Often my clients find other roles in the same organisation or retrain for more suitable occupations – with smaller, more manageable companies, or self-employment perhaps turning a hobby into a career.

## Effects of Trauma and High Sensitivity on the Brain

Trauma can have various effects on the brain, similar to what we saw with sensitivity itself (Figure 6), including the **dopaminergic response/ reward system**. It seems that trauma exacerbates the existing neurological changes with respect to the *meaning of experience*, in particular, emotional memories which is stored in the **insula cortex** of our limbic brain.

### Complex Emotions

There are 3 **complex emotions** which particularly embed themselves – abandonment, betrayal and humiliation, which most children experience at some point in their lives. Death may be perceived as abandonment, but certainly divorce or a parent leaving home will be. Betrayal is the transgression of trust – for instance a parent says if you are good, they will take you out for your birthday as a treat, and then they forget[i]. Humiliation is usually a public dismissal or shaming incident. It could be as simple as a friend

---

[i] Believe it or not, I have many clients where this happened. Parents even forgot it was their birthday completely!

making you the butt of their joke in front of others, or a teacher telling you off in front of the class. These small incidents may be dismissed by parents and teachers as nothing but to the sensitive child they are deeply felt and difficult to overcome.

For many highly sensitive children, support is just not there *reliably*. When there is no buffer to that experience, the child's brain will shut down areas involved with the experience of pleasure and motivation. They may become anxious and depressed with little motivation for exploration or faith in their own ability to succeed. Let's look at why that happens in the context of a trauma response mediated via the dopaminergic reward system. The changes are as follows:

- Hypoactivity in the reward system: Trauma can lead to a decrease in overall activity within the reward system, including reduced dopamine release. This can result in a diminished ability to experience pleasure or motivation, known as **anhedonia**. Individuals may find it difficult to find joy or interest in activities they once enjoyed.
- Altered reward processing: Trauma can disrupt the brain's processing of rewards, leading to an imbalance in the dopaminergic response. This can result in a blunted or exaggerated response to rewarding stimuli. Some individuals may become less responsive to

pleasurable experiences, while others may seek out intense or risky activities in an attempt to feel a heightened sense of reward.

- Hyperarousal and hypervigilance: Trauma can lead to a heightened state of arousal and hypervigilance, characterized by increased sensitivity to potential threats. This heightened state can be associated with increased dopamine release, leading to a constant state of alertness. However, chronic hyperarousal can be exhausting and dysregulate the reward system over time.

- Impaired decision-making: Trauma can interfere with the prefrontal cortex's ability to make balanced and rational decisions, which is an essential part of the reward system. The prefrontal cortex helps regulate and modulate the dopaminergic response, but trauma-related changes can lead to impulsive or dysfunctional decision-making.

Thus, you can see that traumatised children (and the adults they grow up to become are impaired in their emotional and decision making functioning (which it turns out is largely emotional not cognitive). Or they are not able to express their emotions at all (in a state of dissociation, shutdown or freeze). Many times, this will express itself as a lack of self-care, repetitive behaviours that have no positive benefit, and difficulties in relationships. They may find it difficult to trust or deny their bodies or emotional needs. This makes for a problematic adult life, particularly as they will have little awareness of why these patterns keep repeating. So, we see that these little traumas can be very significant for sensitive children. But we need to be a bit more nuanced so that we understand it's not the same pattern for everyone. Trauma is individual as well as societal.

## Neurologically Individual Responses to Trauma

It's important to note that the effects of trauma on the brain and the reward system can vary between individuals. Different types of trauma, its severity, and an individual's resilience and coping mechanisms all play a role in determining the specific impact on the dopaminergic response and other aspects of brain function which we looked at in the previous chapter.

Of course, these changes are linked to the quality of the childhood experience which is a *perception* and thus individual to that child (even children in the same family can have a very different perception of the same events). All highly sensitive children show a decline in the reward area of the brain in response to negative experiences (making them much more prone to addictions in adult life). For more neurotypical children the differential is much smaller as we saw in Chapter 2.

But conversely with positive childhood experience, highly sensitive children do much better than their peers so that differential becomes beneficial. What do we mean by 'positive'? Does it have to be perfect? No. In fact when looking at psychological health, it is not the *absence* of negative experiences per se, but the way they are handled that builds **emotional resilience**.

Let's take an example. Let's go back to the situation we discussed before. A mother needs to leave her child with a childminder (like many mothers have to do – this is not a criticism). How you explain that to a young child depends on their sensitivity as well as age. Most neurotypical children will cope well with that change, provided they know it's temporary i.e., the mother will return. But for sensitive children they may need extra information. So, to explain it's so that mummy can go to work to provide for the family and they'll have more money to do fun things together later[i]. And it's most certainly not because they have been bad i.e., it's not a punishment.

One client of mine remembers clearly the effects of being told by an aunt 'you know this is nothing to do with you, don't you?' about her mother's erratic behaviour. She saw it as supportive because then it

---

[i] This adds connectivity between what is happening now and what will happen later is really important for a sensitive child. You can practice this with school age children dropping them off at school. Not just saying 'see you later' but 'when we'll do <insert fun thing>'. This takes away a lot of anxiety as it adds emotional safety.

wasn't about punishment of her, for not being better/good enough/ able to save her mother in some way. Although in our example, it's clearly not a punishment to be left while mum goes to work, a sensitive child may view it that way. So extra care needs to be taken to normalize their feelings of abandonment. Even if as a parent you think rationally, your child does not. They exhibit magical thinking and won't have a context for the behaviours they are seeing/experiencing. For neurologically sensitive children, they are at the centre of their world and if they are experiencing separation or abandonment, it is because they, somehow, are not good enough.

## Lifelong Psychological Consequences of Adverse Childhood Experience

We have seen that having understanding and support during childhood is vital but what if you grew up without this and were overwhelmed and unsupported. There are lifelong consequences for expression and healthy selfhood:

- Failure to separate/individuate psychologically – so we become enmeshed with others easily.
- Addiction to fixer and peacekeeping roles – to give us validation.
- People-pleasing - our needs can come second to partners/children or parents (we feel invisible/ ignored but seldom stand up for ourselves as we can't take the stress).

- Tendency to isolate ourselves as a means to avoid conflict.
- Overwork/achieve to distract ourselves from the pain of being misunderstood.
- We may be addicted to positivity (itself a form of emotional repression).
- Generalised anxiety (without obvious cause) and even 'borrowed' anxiety from people really close to us – we feel their pain.

These patterns become quite fixed and are even more difficult to resolve if they have been around for decades because they become normalized - they are just 'who we are'! Of course, this is a perception rather than an absolute truth. How are we to know who we could be without the beliefs and experiences we grew up with?

The way in which many of us become aware that we are in some state of dysfunction is that certain patterns start to recur. We keep repeating certain relationship problems with different people. Life is not panning out the way we hoped, or we are stuck in some physical syndrome (chronic pain, anxiety, fatigue) with no obvious way out.

This is usually when people are forced to accept they have a problem and seek help to make some changes. We very seldom spontaneously decide to make changes unless we perceive we are suffering some limitation or pain. That emotional repression can lead to physical issues is only now beginning to be understood. The next chapter examines the more long-term body-based physical effects of a life of a chronic (toxic) stress burden.

CHAPTER FIVE: THE ADVERSE EFFECTS OF HIGH SENSITIVITY

So, we have seen that little things like 'small-t' traumas and unresolved emotional imprints have a big impact for highly sensitive people. The two combine to create a toxic time bomb of unrelenting **toxic stress**. This plays itself out in behavioural ways which become habitual over time. Anxiety (our own and other people's felt by us) becomes our daily bread. And when illness strikes, we are thrown into a horrible downward cycle of worry because our coping strategies of distraction, overwork or emotional denial no longer work.

## Toxic Stress and the Anxiety Loop

We get into the 'anxiety loop', afraid of our own symptoms which no amount of thinking or gathering information seems to fix[i]. Our thinking brains tell us that we *should be able to fix this* and when we can't (and indeed the thinking itself gives us more stress signals

---

[i] ! Both of these have been my 'go-to' when dealing with any sort of challenge in the past but when chronic fatigue struck me in my 30's this no longer worked.

so we get worse with time), we blame ourselves and are scathing and negative in our self-talk. "I'm pathetic, this is ridiculous, I'm just making this up, how stupid I must be if I can't sort this", etc.

These incessant thoughts of failure which lie just beneath the surface, are sometimes corroborated by friends and family who may tell us to 'keep positive, buck up, don't think about it so much" or they may think you're not really ill/suffering because you look ok (these conditions aren't visible), or they may seek to shame us – "look at all the people in the world who have something really to complain about!" We fall into despair as our efforts to assert our truth are denied, belittled or ignored.

What underlies these negative beliefs about what's going on? Why is it that other people are much more sympathetic when it's something obvious like a broken leg or socially supported like a cancer diagnosis? But if you're struggling with hidden conditions of anxiety, panic attacks, dizziness, brain fog, pain or fatigue for which there is no treatment pathway they assume it's 'all in your head'?

The problem is the medical model we currently are treated under – the **biomedical model** sees all disease as organic to the tissue it expresses itself in. To give a simple example – chronic back pain originates in the tissues of the back and thus to treat the problem we must treat the back[i]. But this idea was debunked over 20 years ago by Dr John Sarno in his ground-breaking book Healing Back Pain. He saw that most of the symptoms (apart from acute injuries obviously) were related to suppressed emotions of anger, responsibility, grief and shame. This creates a stress response in the brain and nervous system that limits oxygen and other nutrients to the tissues, creating pain. But nobody looks at what is going on emotionally as a potential driver. They focus on alleviating symptoms only.

The strange truth is that the symptoms are actually *the body's way of trying to resolve the underlying issues of toxic stress,* but we have no way of understanding this. Most of us grow up in an emotionally deprived culture, where 'big boys don't cry' or the standard model of managing is 'keep calm and carry on'. This may enable us to survive our childhoods and the intrinsic powerlessness of that situation but gradually as we hit midlife, we find it less and

---

[i] And even holistic practitioners like chiropractors use this model though they have a broader understanding of complementary practices like nutrition and massage.

less effective. Brene Brown talks about our armour becoming a limitation because like the shell of a snail it can't grow with us!

For highly sensitive people this strategy of ignoring our emotions just doesn't work but serves to drive the problem deeper. As our efforts get more and more desperate, and our coping strategies less and less effective, we get more stuck in the anxiety loop which exacerbates our deeply held beliefs that we are somehow incompetent, making it all up, just not trying hard enough. And this inevitably leads to physical symptoms in the body.

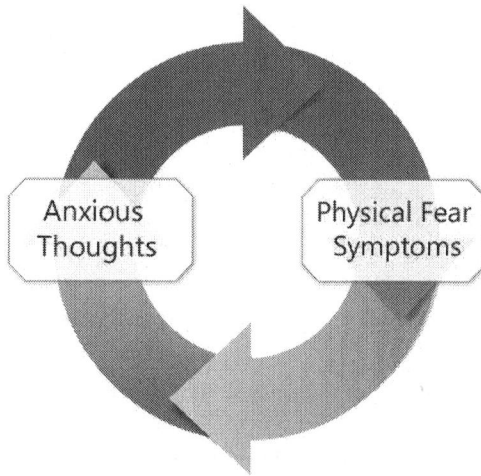

**Figure 14: The Anxiety Loop with Physical Symptoms**

This increased stress of anxious thoughts builds the body's need to gain your attention – so your symptoms tend to go deeper and get more severe with time. As you begin to fear your body's responses/symptoms, the stress deepens, and an ever-increasing circle of symptoms and more anxious fear of symptoms develops. This is the anxiety loop, and it is how people get very stuck in debilitating symptoms for years and even decades if it is not addressed.

We have to break the fear of symptoms by reframing them as the body's communication mechanism – not a sign that things are getting worse physically. The **autonomic nervous system** unfortunately does double duty as both our physiological balance monitoring system (heart-rate, blood pressure, digestive function, etc) *and* our emotional response mechanism. It is linked to both our physical survival and our psychological wellbeing.

What is the issue here? What emotion is underlying this painful and debilitating syndrome? The answer may surprise you – shame.

# Shame – The Hidden Emotion

## What is Shame?

So, what exactly is shame? It's perhaps not an emotion that initially resonates with you.   It is NOT being ashamed of oneself for something you did, that's not what I mean. It's an internal feeling of being out of your depth, unsupported, wrong, bad, not enough that many people have under the surface (covered up sometimes with overachieving, competitive or people-pleasing behaviours[i]). It is incredibly common (I would say most people have some) but because it's not a conscious experience (it sits in the neuronal connections of the limbic and survival brains), we seldom know we have it.

Indeed, for me I wasn't aware at all. I thought I was very capable and mentally strong so couldn't possibly have shame. But an epiphany occurred when I was doing some healing work with Louise Hay's book 'Heal your Life' in my late 30s and was instructed to tell my reflection in the mirror that 'I love you'[ii]. I realised *I simply couldn't meet my own eye gaze* (a really common indicator that

---

[i] Narcissists, interestingly, have huge amounts of internalised shame but no conscious awareness so become controlling and shaming of others as a strategy to dispel the anxiety that wells up in their bodies.

[ii] An exercise encouraged at the end of Chapter 1 of the book Heal Your Life.

indicates shame[i]). What was going on? I suddenly felt a deep wave of some unpleasant feelings, which I had no idea how to label. It was what I now call 'the 'wash of shame' that I had never experienced consciously before, and it bewildered me.

What I learned subsequently was it has nothing to do with what you *did* (that's guilt) but about how you feel about yourself. It was only through reading that book that I came to understand, that shame is not about conscious awareness, but *an unconscious feeling of wrongness*. Shame is about who you believe yourself to be at a fundamentally deep level.

---

[i] When you can't meet your own or other's eye gaze this indicates some internalised shame

## Case Study -Sarah

To give an example from my practice let's look at Sarah, a young 27-year-old woman with her whole life ahead of her. But she is unable to leave her parent's house, wracked with chronic pain in all areas of her body (diagnosed as Fibromyalgia) and lives on a cocktail of antidepressants and sleeping tablets to numb the body so she can sleepi.

Social interactions are physically painful for her, so she limits them, friends have to come and visit her and her obvious pain and suffering mean that these visits become less and less as friends inevitably drop away. Having a relationship is out of the question. The last one she had ended so badly that she couldn't face another, even if she did have the physical energy! She is living in a limbo of suffering even though physically doctors can't find anything wrong with her. She begins truly believing it's all in her head and she has created this issue somehow to gain attention or avoid her lifei.

However, when we delve deeper, we find an issue in her early childhood which enabled a long hospitalization without her parents, and social awkwardness from that moment on, which she pushed through even to the point of putting herself in dangerous and isolated environments. When we are able to heal the unresolved emotions of that experience which she can't even remember, we can help her to face what her body has been telling her all these years.

When Sarah learns that she is alone and inadequate in the face of stress, although she battles to deny it – even moving to another country to work to prove herself! Being in denial of the danger this presents as she is away from her friends and family in as isolated place, and she then has an abuse experience at work which forces her to return. This engenders tremendous shame as she has failed (again!), to be 'normal' and now has the sexual shame of being violated on top of this.

Sarah continued

And so begins the toxic stew of internal shame. It's an emotion that embeds itself silently in her body and begins to give her digestive issues, allergies which develop over time into panic attacks, heart irregularities and insomnia. Her parents do not know what is wrong and she cannot tell them. Admitting her failure to make an independent life was simply too much to bear.

In order to get out of this, we had to allow her to be witnessed in her vulnerability, to know that what happened to her wasn't her fault and to be able to soothe her body in new ways that reassure her and the traumatized child within and calm the stress response in her limbic brain. This type of healing is relational because the original trauma was relational, and it works in the same part of the brain that registers safety – your emotional/limbic brain. You must have relational safety for this to work. That's why working with a practitioner often makes a big difference. But not any practitioner – this must be done with someone you feel gets you emotionally.

Luckily for Sarah, she and I clicked, and the soothing worked, slowly but surely, the unwinding was gentle (some people have sudden catharses, but for others this is a gradual process). She is now on the road to recovery and understands that validating her emotions and self-soothing are important life skills.

# Shame and Vulnerability - Brené Brown

Shame researcher Brené Brown has done extensive research on this which I won't repeat here. I refer you to her wonderful TED talks and books on the subject (see Bibliography) where she describes how she found that shame is a common experience for many children where their emotional needs were not met reliably for all sorts of reasons (often linked with 'small t' traumas like being different to siblings, bullying or being disliked or outcast from the family).

She and her team interviewed thousands of people and discovered something shocking: that shame was common and overcoming it was about acknowledging it not denying it! A wholehearted life consisted of facing your unwitnessed emotions in the eyes of a safe other, and not repressing them. This so shocked Brené that she went into therapy herself, and now makes a living from talking about shame and its imprints and helping people to live better lives. I highly recommend her work and approach. She is very warm and funny, so it's a joy to watch her talk.

## Shame Arises from Trauma and Sensitivity Combined

In many ways shame is linked with trauma (if you define trauma as anything that overwhelms you), as it is the *learned experience of yourself in a state of overwhelm in that traumatic event*. If you were sexually abused, or ignored, left to fend for yourself, or perhaps you had to parent your parent or siblings because of your parents' emotional inadequacy, that teaches us that we are not enough. No child can fully replace a responsible caring adult and so it's not because you were inadequate but that you had too much responsibility too young. You were vulnerable without support.

Why have I included shame here and not in the previous chapter? Because *shame is a body-based experience*, it's not a cognitive one, but a feeling of being alone, unwelcome, not enough in the world somehow. And it can be induced by experiences common to many childhoods. Birth trauma, inability to breastfeed or be soothed by mother, surgeries (particularly those that involved anaesthetic[i]), treatments or situations that involve being separated or isolated like divorce or parental separation. The antidote to shame is connection to a safe, validating other and luckily for us it can help even many years later.

## Shame Imprints in Adult Life

What is shame important? What if you simply don't think you have any? I didn't. I believed shame was about having done bad things deliberately. But that's not what shame is. Shame is a *learned body experience of not feeling enough* or that your needs can be reliably

---

[i] Medical anaesthesia is a form of forced immobilisation of the body which the back brain still records even though the front (cortex) does not. The body has been overwhelmed without a chance to dissipate the energies of the fight and flight stress response.. See The Scar that Won't Heal for more info on this.

met. It is not about being ashamed of yourself, remember. The reason it is important is because it plays out in adulthood in behaviours and coping strategies that limit wellbeing and life purpose. See if you recognise any of these.

The main ways in which adult shame can manifest are:

- **Secrecy and hiding**: adults who experience shame often try to hide their perceived flaws or vulnerabilities. They may keep secrets, avoid sharing their true feelings or experiences, or create a façade or pretence to present themselves as perfect or invulnerable.
- **Perfectionism**: shame can drive adults to pursue perfection in various aspects of their lives. They may set impossibly high standards for themselves, constantly striving to avoid mistakes or failure. The fear of being judged or criticized can be a driving force behind this perfectionistic behavior which often ends in burnout.
- **People-pleasing**: those grappling with shame may constantly seek validation and approval from others. They may prioritize meeting others' expectations, even at the expense of their own needs and values. The fear of rejection or disapproval can drive them to put others' needs before their own.
- **Blaming and deflecting**: a common response to shame is to often try to shift blame onto others or external circumstances. They may find it difficult to take responsibility for their actions or face the consequences of their mistakes. Blaming others can be a way to protect themselves from the discomfort of shame. Narcissists have extreme shame but often deflect onto others particularly partners or children.

- **Isolation and withdrawal**: commonly, shame can lead people to isolate themselves from others. They may withdraw from social interactions, avoiding relationships or activities that could potentially expose their vulnerabilities. Isolation provides a sense of safety by minimizing the chances of being judged or criticized. But it also creates huge loneliness and depression as we are designed to connect with others for good mental health.

- **Comparison and envy**: Shame can fuel a constant need for comparison with others. Adults may feel inadequate or inferior when comparing themselves to others' achievements, appearance, or status. Envy and jealousy can arise as they believe that others are better or more deserving.

- **Self-criticism and denigration**: Individuals experiencing shame often have an inner critical voice that constantly berates and judges them. They may engage in negative self-talk, perpetuating feelings of unworthiness and inadequacy. This self-criticism reinforces and intensifies the experience of shame but because it's all unconscious they may not be aware.

Of course, these are basic principles, and each person manifests them in unique ways. Of more significance to the highly sensitive people that I work with, is the fact that shame changes your physiology so that rest and repair are hijacked.

It is a message of cellular degradation, breakdown and immune system dysregulation[i]. Hence you are at greater risk of developing anxiety and depression (which is linked to signals of inflammation in the brain and other parts of the body). This is all exacerbated when you have experienced adverse circumstances (especially in childhood). This is why Adverse Childhoood Experiences (ACEs) and SPS go hand in hand to create physical symptoms. But not all ACEs are equal and not all people experience them the same way.

## Shame Experiences

Particular experiences that shame us are the complex responses to abandonment, betrayal and humiliation, which occur throughout childhood but are not traumatic when appropriately supported.

Remember trauma is about *being alone with the experience* which creates a feeling of overwhelm which the nervous system memorises as a pattern that will be retriggered if something about the sensory experience is similar (time of year, emotion being felt, tone of voice or sound of something in the environment, etc).

---

[i] In extreme form this is the Cell Danger Response which shuts down your cellular energy metabolism to the lowest state required to keep you alive. I believe this is the basis of chronic fatigue and pain states.

In adulthood reliving these experiences is often what triggers the childhood pattern of shameful beliefs and behaviours to manifest as a shutdown of normal rest and repair mechanisms

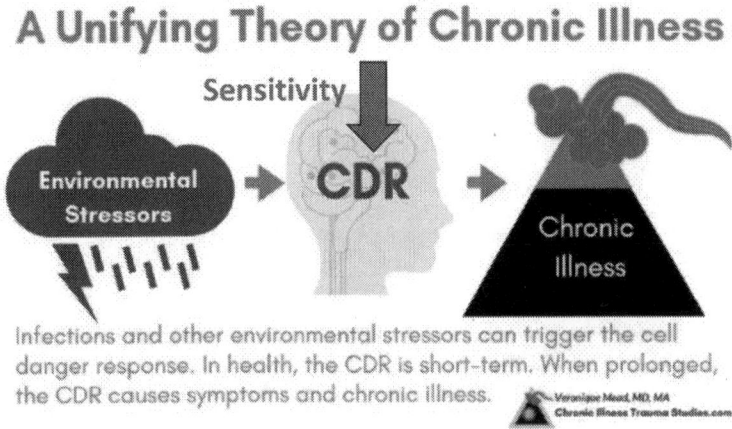

**Figure 15: Cell Danger Response – thanks to V. Mead**

Let me give you an example to illustrate this better.

## Case Study – Pritti

Pritti had a childhood of almost unendurable emotional starvation. Her mother had, as she describes it, 'an undiagnosed borderline personality disorder' and would be completely erratic in her responses. Sometimes resorting to verbal or physical outbursts, she forced her and her older sister to often stay in their rooms for days at a time or beat them if they tried to resist her. Her father was often working or staying out late as he had no interest in them or her mother. He also drank heavily and would often return drunk and abusive. Pritti looked to her older sister to provide what little parenting was available.

But given her sister was equally just a child, this was not really enough to provide what was needed and when her sister left to go to university, Pritti was left on her own with her mother's unpredictable and violent moods. Somehow, she survived and eventually escaped herself into the first relationship that seemed to offer sanctuary. But when that turned out to be abusive too, she had no-one to turn to in order to support her through the breakup and had to take a job that she didn't enjoy just to survive, which she stayed in for years, not really knowing what else to do[i]. She lived alone and had just a few friends as she didn't feel like she could trust many people, particularly women (unfortunately the result of her mother's unpredictability).

Then, when covid struck, she was suddenly without the social support that having a job gives and found herself in lockdown without anyone to help her. She struggled to feed and wash herself, such was the severity of her illness, yet she was not ill enough for a hospital admission, so she struggled on feeling increasingly isolated and abandoned (an echo of her childhood). And when lockdown ended, the symptoms, although not as severe as the initial illness, did not abate – she found herself with a diagnosis of 'long covid'.

## Case Study – Pritti continued

When her coping strategy of emotional denial (a sort of frozen emotional response) became overwhelmed, she found herself in floods of tears for no reason and nobody to help process the horrific experience she had gone through and give her hope for a recovery. She was stuck and knew she needed to change something.

By giving Pritti a safe space to finally feel the deprivation of her childhood (to allow and soothe her unshed tears), we were able to allow her nervous system to resolve those experiences as over. Then we could teach her to soothe and nurture herself emotionally, by listening to her body as a source of information and safety. We identified her high sensitivity was an important part of her and allowed that intuitive emotional part to be expressed. As we did this over a number of weeks and months, she gradually got more energy and found herself able to contemplate going back to work. Albeit with a new company and a different approach where she was able to ask for her needs to be met and bring joy and spontaneity back into her life.

Had Pritti experienced a positive childhood, her sensitivity rewarded, she would have never gone into the kind of job where she was just seen as a cog in a machine. She might have been more inclined towards the arts or a creative industry instead of financial services, to which she was attracted because it was safe. With a positive support model, her brain would have thrived, and reward areas in her brain grown more neuronal connections! She would have had the ability to regulate her emotional responses, a much higher regard for herself and her needs and would have learned to be more assertive about expecting them to be met.

But it's never too late to rewire! With the support and attunement of a good therapist, Pritti learned how to process her emotional upsets and reduce the shame imprints of **rumination** and **hyper-fixation** which were her 'go-to'. She is now able to be in the world knowing she has a place, a purpose and that she is enough after all. She is now considering becoming a therapist herself as she wishes to 'pay it forward' with all that she has learned and help others in the same situation as her. She looks totally different too – her face has lost the stressful look it always had, and her ADHD symptoms are much less.

# Chapter Six – Challenges and Advantages of High Sensitivity

With the understanding that shame embeds itself in the body and mind of the highly sensitive child much more readily than the neurotypical person, we can release the shame imprints and learn to navigate the world in novel ways.

First, we need to understand the special challenges we face and how to mitigate these, then we can look at how we can thrive given the right environment.

It's important to note that while Sensory Processing Sensitivity can present both advantages and disadvantages, the impact of this trait varies from person to person. Each individual's experience of being highly sensitive is unique, influenced by various factors such as their environment, upbringing, and other personality traits. Understanding and embracing these characteristics can help people navigate their sensitivities and accentuate the advantages while mitigating the challenges effectively.

# The Challenges of Emotional Sensitivity.

There is no doubt that being emotionally sensitive presents challenges to living well in a neurotypical world.

We are so easily overwhelmed by strong stimulus (noise, lights, textures), particularly if they are conflicting or competing. Being in a loud, noisy environment like a large supermarket or conference with all the different sounds, harsh lighting and brands vying for your attention can be overstimulating to the point where it exhausts you. A restaurant that has hard floors with a lot of echo and too bright lighting can put you off your food. People with shrill or loud voices can induce a sense of aversion, so that you will naturally move away or want to turn the volume down (if it's possible to do so!).

We are particularly sensitive to noise – it is one of the first senses to come online in the foetus and apparently one of the last to go when we die. People with long-term chronic conditions often report extreme noise sensitivity to the point where they have to wear earplugs. Light sensitivity is also another feature and may require dark glasses to make moving around possible. Vestibular (balance) sensitivity is extremely common and may be triggered by emotional upsets or conflicts. Migraines may also be more common in sensitive people because both are controlled by your autonomic nervous system, and this is typically dysregulated where there has been trauma or lack of emotional support. Modern medicine has no explanation for many of these common ailments – indeed they are often termed 'medically unexplained symptoms' or MUS. That's because the model does not include the nervous system control of most internal body systems (via the autonomic nervous system). People are left with no real solution other than to suppress the symptoms with drugs, but these often have side effects that lead to other symptoms. It is a roller coaster ride with no end.

## Food, Medication and Supplement Sensitivity

One of the strangest effects of a heightened nervous system response is sensitivity to certain foods or medications, which other people do not struggle with. I'm not talking necessarily about gluten or lactose intolerance (though these may occur and often early on), but strange intolerances to foods that develop in sequence. You may start off with a reaction to strawberries for instance and that broadens to most red fruit[i], or you find you cannot tolerate wheat and then all grains become a problem. Or one food in particular becomes such a stressor that you can't even smell it or see others eating it without feeling anxious. People end up with increasingly restricted diets which cause further stress – making the sensitivities even worse.

Medications at standard dose have to be halved or reduced to the barest minimum to have a beneficial effect. Otherwise. the negative side effects become intolerable. The same is true of supplements – vitamins and co-factors that are supposed to help your digestion or cellular functioning for instance, are reacted to – much to the despair of your doctor or practitioner. Many of my clients have this issue which usually means they are sent my way because a nutritional therapist has run out of options to help the person and they realise that there might be something underneath the reactivity that could be detrimental to progress[ii].

---

[i] If you think I am exaggerating here I knew a lady who was allergic to all red foods! They caused terrible insomnia, and it took doctors ages to work out what it was that was making her sleep so difficult. How is this possible? It is a complex association.
[ii] Here I am specifically referring to the effects of trauma on top of the natural sensitivity.

You may be intolerant of the smell of normal household chemicals: fabric softeners, air fresheners, paints and perfumes. Maybe like me you are allergic to metals, latex or certain fabrics on the skin. These reactions are part and parcel of the nature of heightened sensitivity because of the way the brain interprets mild stimuli as strong sensory inputs as we saw in an earlier chapter.

## Electrical sensitivity

For many years we have struggled to understand why some people are especially electrically sensitive. But undoubtedly there are some people who are affected by Electromagnetic Fields (EMFs including Wi-Fi, dirty electrical fields around old wiring, etc) and I am certain there is some crossover with food sensitivity and sensitivity in general. There are various theories why this may occur including anaemia and lack of zinc but because the symptoms are often neurological (and especially autonomic), I feel that it is worth considering environmental sensitivity of the HSP to be an important factor. Here are the common symptoms related to EMF exposure:

- Musculoskeletal: pain, spasms, vibration
- Respiratory: pressure in ears, tooth pain, tightness in chest, shortness of breath

- Cardiovascular: palpitation, flushing, tachycardia, edema
- Gastrointestinal: belching, nausea
- Ocular: burning pain in eyes, teariness
- Neurological: tingling, sleepiness, headaches, dizziness, loss of consciousness
- Dermal: itching, burning, prickly pain

Note the variety and seeming unrelated symptoms which make no sense unless we consider the **autonomic nervous system**, in particular the vagus and cranial nerves as the controlling factor.

## The Vagus Nerve

The vagus in particular is drawing a lot of attention these days[i]. It is in fact two nerves (the upper of ventral vagus) and its associated cranial nerves around the head face and neck, and the dorsal vagus which largely innervates the internal organs. The latter is mostly controlling processes over which we have little or no voluntary control: breathing, digestion, heart rate and even immunity.

---

[i] Apart from being very trendy on social media it is drawing a lot of scientific interest – a Guardian article drew attention to the international research going on into different ways to rebalance it:
https://www.theguardian.com/society/2023/aug/23/the-key-to-depression-obesity-alcoholism-and-more-why-the-vagus-nerve-is-so-exciting-to-scientists.

When these nerves are out of balance multiple symptoms begins to appear like dizziness, IBS/IBD, POTS[i] and various auto-immune diseases like Rheumatoid Arthritis, Sjogren's, Lupus, etc.

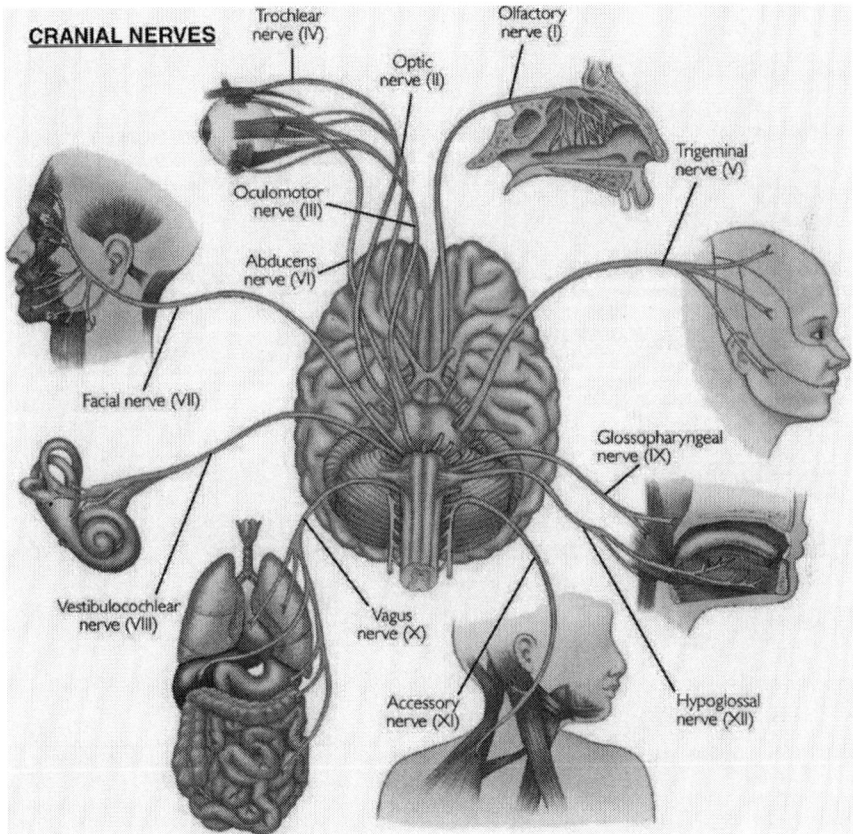

**Figure 16: Autonomic Vagal Nerve Controls the Body**

---

[i] Postural Orthostatic Tachycardia Syndrome – where they blood pressure drops rather than rises upon standing causing dizziness.

## Psychological Triggers

It's not just physical stimuli that get interpreted as a threat. Mental/ emotional conflicts or difficulties can also be very triggering for highly sensitive people. We are highly conflict avoidant in general (whereas some people actively seem to enjoy a good argument we are likely to walk away and avoid such a scene). So, any implied criticism or negative facial expressions (whether intended or not) such as people frowning, looking cross (which we will largely interpret as being cross with *us*) or not responding in ways that we anticipate can potentially cause deep anxiety. We get used to pretending we're alright and hiding our distress but the physiological effects on the body happen anyway.

We can also be triggered around people with strong personalities, loud or grating voices, who make big gestures, explosive comments, etc. People with stressed/ traumatized energies can also make us feel very uncomfortable. I can remember hiding behind my mother when being introduced to such people in the street. There was also an auntie who had a really loud laugh who used to terrify me. I thought it was everyone who felt this way but of course most people don't take that amount of sensory information in, and their brains fail to enact the stress response, therefore. Sensory processing sensitivity heightens the depth of processing remember so we feel things more acutely than neurotypical people.

## Navigating Relationships

Addressing the unique challenges and dynamics that highly sensitive individuals may encounter in various relationships is an important life skill. By relationships I include family, friendships, romantic partnerships, and workplace interactions. They all take skill to navigate well and sadly in this, as in so many things, our education is rather lacking. Emotional intelligence is not something taught routinely in schools, whose focus is on the practical and academic skill set. In sexual relationships, we can feel very vulnerable and are often at risk of being overwhelmed by strong emotions, leading to difficulties in communication and conflict resolution.

Let's look at an example of one of my clients:

## Case Study – Vicky

Vicky is a highly sensitive working mum - she feels like she can never win with her family. She tries to do all the right things by everyone, being compliant and dedicating herself to others, but the resentment keeps spilling over and she has occasional aggressive outbursts which her husband tries to soothe. Then she feels terribly guilty afterwards as she can see that he and the children are picking up on her stress even though she's trying to keep it under wraps. She keeps all the plates spinning but loses herself, mired in terrible fatigue. It gets to the point where she can no longer go on holiday as she fears having a crash with her ME symptoms and so would rather not be a 'burden' as she puts it.

Even though she benefits hugely from the support she gets in our sessions, she fails to reach out when she needs extra help between sessions (the childhood pattern of her needs not being met means she cannot trust anyone will be there for her). When reminded that she has someone she can reach out to (who is not emotionally involved with her in the same way as her partner for instance), she is able to feel less alone and hopeless.

By showing her the nature of implicit (unconscious) memory, she begins to see the debilitating symptoms she experienced on her last holiday were triggered by a memory of a childhood holiday where she had a major life-threatening asthma attack after a stay in a damp, mouldy cottage triggered her. The panic and extreme stress she witnessed in her mother on the way home (with the feeling of emergency and guilt over ruining her mother's holiday), has buried itself in her body without her knowing. When we are able to release that memory as being over instead of in the ever-present 'now', her body can relax on holiday, and she can stop avoiding them. She begins to build trust that she can change things for the better and build her own mental and physical resources so that she can be part of her family again.

Our vulnerability to criticism whether deliberate or implied means some of us will likely turn to people pleasing behaviours, in order to make it less likely. We end up sacrificing our own needs for the needs of others in ways that become habitual and then we can feel terrific resentment afterwards which we bury in our bodies.

Another area that sensitives can find challenging is change. Sudden endings are particularly hard for us, whether at the end of a relationship, job or moving home, the sudden loss of familiarity is perceived as a threat. Interestingly, our fear centre, the amygdalae (remember there are two of them below the hypothalamus in the emotional brain) are actually triggered by many things not just straightforward fearful situations. We can be triggered by unfamiliarity. We may get used to dysfunctional relationships and the loss of them, even though we know rationally as needed, will be registered by the amygdala as a threat. Hence why we may stay longer in unsatisfactory situations than we ought to.

Indeed, we take relationships really seriously – we cannot shrug off problems or let them wash over us. We are very hurt by misunderstandings, judgements, or injustice – particularly false accusations. At school I have never forgotten being shamed for something I did not do and being forced to stand for hours in the playground after others had gone into lessons. Shame is not a good behavioural adjustment method for highly sensitive people as they already have a strong sense of duty and moral rightness, so shaming only embeds the idea what they have failed again. I also have a memory of my mother accusing me of locking the front door at night (which I denied, in tears). One day I caught her doing it by habit (she was not aware she was doing it) and felt relieved that I was right after all. She was very sorry of course, and a little embarrassed, but I was still very hurt she would not believe me when I said I didn't do it. It affected my trust in her emotionally.

## Intimacy and Pleasure

Our heightened sensitivity can make us more susceptible to feeling overwhelmed or overstimulated during intimate moments, leading to potential challenges in physical intimacy. For some that will mean avoiding intimacy completely (there is actually a gender identity now that includes those who consider themselves 'asexual'. I wonder how many are actually highly sensitive people who had trauma in their upbringing?[i]) For others it will mean shutting down

---

[i] Remember these two together are what can inhibit good neurological functioning.

at crucial moments leaving their partner feeling confused and rejected. Sexual response needs a well-balanced autonomic nervous system as arousal and orgasm is a complex interplay between the active and passive arousal systems of the parasympathetic system (fight, flight and freeze respectively).

We are highly attuned morally so people who lie or fail to follow through with their promises will hurt us deeply – even if it is someone we hardly know. To give an example – a plumber promises to come and fix your bathroom but fails to answer your calls or promises to come on a certain date and doesn't turn up. This is annoying for anyone, but for the highly sensitive this is a deep betrayal of the trust we have put in them, and it cuts deeply.

Or a friend who we have trusted to always be there for us suddenly cuts us off or turns against us. We may find ourselves ruminating on this for days and weeks afterwards due to our depth of processing. We think about something deeply before acting and cannot understand why others act rashly or without consideration for others. As an example, a highly sensitive solicitor client of mine recalls being ignored for promotion at work in favour of a more junior colleague, and she can't let it go. It rankles because it's unjust given how much work she put into the company. At the same time a friend she trusted stabs her in the back and tells other friends lies about her so that she is excluded from the group. She goes over and over this in her mind to the point it makes her ill. Her family tell her to let if go but she finds this very hard.

Because we are generally self-effacing, and other-oriented we can feel over responsible for the problems of others. If this is the case and we are helpless to intervene, we may struggle internally with a sense of failure. In some ways this is using our childlike magical thinking patterns to decide it must be our fault! This does not happen consciously, we will rationalize that we did all we could, but underneath our stomach/ guts will be churning or locked into spasm.

## Highly Sensitive People and Narcissists

One final point worth emphasizing is that highly sensitive people (with high empathy) can be east targets for narcissists (people low on the empathy scale with a need to control). I see clients over and over who have been stuck in controlling relationships whether with partners or friends who use them to bolster their own lack of self-esteem and then blame the sensitive for any problems (gaslighting).

This is a huge subject of its own with many, many skilled therapists who help people extricate themselves from such relationships by dealing with the underlying cause – a belief that only you can change that person for the better (an impossible feat) by being nicer/ more productive/ trying harder, etc. This is a treadmill that you will never get off unless you deal with what is in YOU that is not resolved and your need to be loved being tied to your worthiness to exist. Once you are able to truly embrace that you are worthy unconditionally, you have less need to prove yourself worthy by over-giving.

## Professional and Career Considerations

Of course, our relationships are not just personal ones. Most of us spend at least a third of our time at work and our work relationships may be equally challenging.

High sensitivity is not acknowledged in most workplaces, and everyone is expected to cope similarly with the environment. But we aren't neurologically the same, so it makes no sense to expect we're all going to have the same responses.

Coping with Overstimulation: Strategies and Techniques

Large open plan offices with mobile 'hot' desking options are terrible places for the highly sensitive. We need to feel we belong and have a conducive environment in order to be able to concentrate or our brains will be constantly picking up the noise, the hum of chatter and machines. Although we will push through to ignore this, the constant stimulation will be registered physiologically.

Also, highly active environments with people coming and going are highly dysregulating. Many people seem to thrive in these environments, but highly sensitive people will struggle. Sadly, due to the inherent problems we experienced as children when under-supported, we often get addicted to the stress signals and feel very attracted to jobs that give us the adrenaline buzz. That doesn't mean its sustainable or desirable!

Thus, finding compatible work environments that allow us to be part of a small team, or working for ourselves where we can manage our tasks better can be attractive options.

## Sensory Self-care - Creating Calm Environments

Learning to notice the warning signs when we are not managing stress on the job very well, finding time out and places that help harmonize us is essential. When I worked in a large university department office, I would take regular breaks out in the botanic garden to get some nature time. It always restored me.

Finding a role that suits you is also essential – you cannot as a highly sensitive person have any job – it won't be enough like it is for most people. You need to have something that gives you meaning and purpose, that matches your values and yet is sustainable. Find out what your values are[i] and leverage your strengths for career success. It's tempting to do a role that is almost right for you, but getting career coaching or therapy to find out what it is you need will help you enormously. I often say to my clients, you don't need a job, you need a vocation! The term vocation means calling and it is a wonderful restorative message to your body when you're doing something you really love and are good at. Let's look at an example:

---

[i] You can do an online values exercise to find out what your values are – it's very important to know and it may turn out different to what you imagine. I always thought health was my top value, but it turns out that authenticity trumps that every time. Finding a job that matches these can take time, but it will be worth it.

## Case Study - Jessica

Jessica is a gifted artist – so much so that she came top of her graduate class and was headhunted by a prestigious design company to lead their design team straight out of college. But the work environment was terrible – full of competitive artists all trying to outdo each other and her male bosses took advantage of Jessica's naivety and one in particular was nasty and manipulative to the point of abusive. She found herself dreading going in and eventually had to resign because the stress was simply too much. She never returned to art choosing instead to go into administration until her children were born and then she decided to focus on being a full-time mum, with the idea of being an 'earth mother'. But the traumatic birth of her first child wiped that dream away.

As a mother, she found her children took increasing amounts of her time and energy and as her confidence diminished, she started to think of herself as a failure. Her body became wracked with pain.

Although we wouldn't want to return her to that toxic work environment, we do want to encourage her to find her creative instinct again. I asked her to start experimenting by painting her emotions particularly her rage and to recognise that her talent was never held in high esteem by her family so in many ways she was set up to flounder. By getting back in touch with her spirit, she is able to begin to imagine herself as a creative being and her pain begins to reduce and her energy to return.

## Setting healthy boundaries

Most sensitives have highly porous boundaries – it's a product of our extreme empathy! We are not always sure whose emotions we are feeling. When my mother was ill with dementia, it felt like *me* who was experiencing the pain of her not remembering things. In work situations this means when people are upset or angry, we absorb those emotions too. Imagine if you're working in a department with 20 people, most of whom are miserable or angry! Sadly, that's often the cases with poor management which is rife[i].

And if you are one of those sensitives who grew up trying to be like everyone else and adopted a pushing through coping strategy, you'll likely find your body will pay the price. Learning not to take on too much – saying 'no' to excess work or tasks that are not in your remit is vital.

---

[i] In my experience good managers are a rare thing, People are often promoted to managing roles to which they are entirely unsuited. Usually, this is because they have simply been around long enough or were good at a particular role and then the decision to promote them is made, or they take it on to ensure career progression. That was the case in many of the different public and private arenas I've worked in. But good management requires an aptitude for people which is often entirely missing!

# The Positive Aspects of High Sensitivity

Despite all the challenges we face, high sensitivity is not to be considered a problem. It does, after all, confer advantages on the person with sensory processing sensitivity.

## Emotional Sensitivity and Empathy

First and foremost, our incredible empathy – something we take for granted as normal[i]. We can mirror others' emotions instinctively, sometimes taking on too much (our boundaries can be poor) but because we feel things acutely, we are able to accurately determine an individual's mental/emotional state without asking. We study the body language of that person without conscious awareness – it's an inbuilt mechanism that we are taking in information on an unconscious level to assess its meaning. Whether we recognise that and use it (as many therapists and counsellors do) or we are just connecting with others, it's a laudable skill. It makes us great in caring professions, although burnout can also result if we're not careful in erecting our boundaries.

---

[i] Indeed, some are extremely sensitive people who score very high on the HSP scale and are termed empaths.

We have an uncanny ability to detect atmospheres/ unspoken feeling in a room or situation – this makes us great barometers of safety. Indeed, in the tribes we would have once belonged to, we would have been the lookouts in the tribe – sent to scout out a new environment or new tribe. In modern day life that is less apparently useful, but it comes into its own when looking at work situations to assess suitability and matching person to role for instance. We make great HR people too!

We generally have a nose for inauthenticity – people (politicians) who are 'economical with the truth' or self-serving and hypocrisy. We like to speak the truth to power and serve fairness in all things.

We have a need for quiet time to reflect/ regroup after busy periods or contact with overwhelming people or situations. If we push through although it will seem like we're coping well, our bodies will crash soon after. Quiet time doesn't necessarily mean resting – it could be walking in the woods, baking, crafts or gardening. It means time doing something which uses our procedural memory rather than frontal cortex (thinking brain)

It offends us deeply when we see people or animals being hurt or abused. Even reading about it in the news becomes difficult to process and many sensitives will avoid watching the news, as it becomes too overwhelming neuro-physiologically. We have to get more of a balance with positive information, or we become frozen with our inability to help. This may play out in feeling depressed, dissociated (disconnected from our feelings) as well as upset, so it's often not that easy to recognise.

## The Empath – An Extremely Highly Sensitive Person

Empaths are the top 10% of so of the high sensitivity spectrum but the vast majority of people who come for therapy because not only do they have the sensory sensitivity but also, they feel too much empathy and find it difficult to cope either mentally or physically (or both!).

They struggle because not only do they feel too much within their own experience, but they also *absorb others' emotions and physical symptoms into their own bodies*! This is a problem because they are never free to be in their own experience without overwhelm. When you are simply downloading all the problems of everyone around you, there is no filter on experience, and it is totally overwhelming.

They are emotional sponges so absorb and feel even more than most highly sensitive people so often burnout or crash. So, they need extra tools to deal with their empathy or they are susceptible to panic attacks, depression or exhaustion from taking too much on.

There are a variety of different types of empaths with highly intuitive abilities as psychiatrist and empath Judith Orloff states:

- Earth empaths
- Plant empaths
- Animal empaths (e.g., horse or dog whisperers)
- Mediumship empaths (clairvoyants/sentients)

Although I have some of these features (I feel an animal's pain for example and often attract wounded animals), empaths often tune into different levels of existence so often live in different planes to most of us. Let's take an example:

## Case Study - Sarah

Sarah has always taken on the emotions and pain of her mother. Born into a highly religious family, she was expected to assuage the sins of those around her by being a good girl, but not only that her parents expected total dedication to a life of religious purification (denial of the flesh, suffering in order to rise to heaven, etc). But Sarah although gifted in musically was also prone to acts of clairvoyance which was very disconcerting to her parents (who regarded that as the devil's work!), and she was packed off to a boarding school for musically gifted children.

This should have been a wonderful experience for Sarah but was abusive and alienating. Her extreme empathic sensitivity was ridiculed and feared and so she was subject to the worst forms of bullying like being pushed down some stone steps where she broke her coccyx. She didn't dare tell anyone about this or how much pain she was in as she knew that identifying the perpetrators would result in worse treatment.

She has lifelong trauma from that experience and suffers with debilitating physical symptoms relating to embodied shame (difficulties meeting eye contact, eating and absorption issues, muscle weakness, pain and fatigue)[i]. These are all trauma symptoms and are being gradually resolved by working through the memories somatically so that they are no longer in her body.

We also welcome her visions and show her that these are profoundly spiritual experiences and nothing to be feared. She begins to trust she can be loved just as she is.

There is a spectrum of empathy – narcissists on one end (no empathy), middle (most people), then the higher 20% sensitive to sound, light and smells and the top 10% of those (with scores over 24 in the HSP scale) who I would class as empaths.

They have highly developed intuitive abilities that they have usually learned to deny e.g., being able to connect with dead people, past lives or get intuitive messages from plants or animals. This can often be so overwhelming that they find it hard to be present in their bodies as their minds are constantly taking them on journeys into other planes of existence! Many grew up in families where they were recognised as sensitive but told to 'toughen up' and their abilities ridiculed or suppressed. It was certainly not ok to admit you got messages from entities or spirits!

The degree of connectedness to others (even dead others) seems to be a result of the attunement functioning of your pineal gland. A tiny spiral gland in the centre of your brain, it is directly linked to empathic connection with spirit/ god/ the bigger picture[i]. Most children have highly developed empathy, but by the time they're 7 the pineal is already beginning to calcify and harden which limits these abilities.

---

[i] Perhaps also the source of Extra-sensory Perception (ESP).

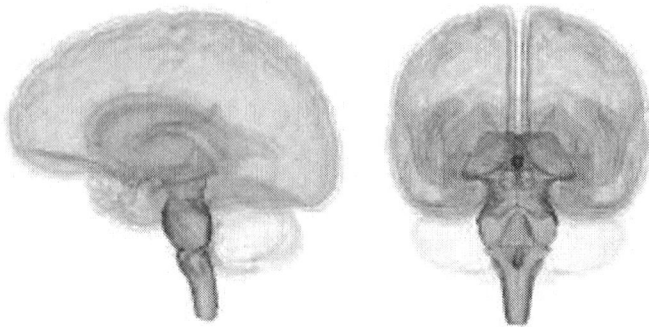

**Figure 17: Pineal Gland – Source of High Empathy**

There are other parts of your brain which are also involved – the insula cortex is also implicated (see Figure 12) and this is often linked to pain perception. So you can imagine that highly sensitive people, who have over-empathised with others' pain (vicarious trauma) often end up with chronic pain syndromes. So much of this expression is unconscious though so it may not always be understood as such.

Empathic abilities are not necessarily fixed though, but it can vary throughout your lifetime, depending on the support you get. Empaths have to understand their special gifts and not be embarrassed about them.

## Examining the Emotional Aspects of High Sensitivity

Whilst we have discussed many of the advantages in terms of neurological differences and sensitivities, there is a deeper aspect that needs to be appreciated and that is the importance of emotional processing.

We are highly emotional creatures, apart from high empathy we also feel things deeply in terms of aesthetics. Aesthetic sensitivity (appreciation of art, music, poetry, landscape, fine food, and so on) is a particularly common feature of the highly sensitive. This means we may be very affected by the arts; it can lift us up to the highest highs and that state may persist for a long time afterwards. We may even be artistic ourselves – we are highly imaginative, full of wonder and awe for the world we inhabit, and creative to the core. This may be expressed as being a great musician, artist, writer or it could be that we are able to be creative in business, our community or the natural world.

## Attunement in Relationships

Our ability to attune to others means we can relate to people (nature and animals) deeply and care about others' feelings (though that can be a double-edged sword as I have already alluded to). But it gives us an undoubted advantage with anticipating other's needs and being a good friend and partner.

Relationships need an attunement to others' shifting moods and priorities which we undoubtedly excel at. This gives us flexibility of response, which is the true meaning of response-ability. It shouldn't necessarily mean a burden, but the ability to choose our response in adaptive ways. I always tell my clients that growing up with an anxious mother was the best training possible for being a therapist as I became adept at reading her moods via subtle face or postural changes. Now I use that ability to read when people are making internal shifts psychologically. The body reads the mind (and actually informs it).

In our relationship with ourselves we tend towards self-reflection and thus don't do things by halves. We often analyse our own and others' motivations (sometimes we go over the top with this to our detriment) but once we have decided to make a change, we generally stick to it. Our ability to make positive changes is unrivalled therefore, once we have given ourselves time to process fully the implications.

## Work and Play

We are often drawn to 'making a difference' in our lives which means we need a meaningful vocation[i] not just a job. Other people can live for the weekend and put up being miserable or unsatisfied in their jobs, but we need to be able to love what we do and put all our creativity into it. It may take us years to work this out, and find the career that works for us, but prioritizing a good work environment if we can, is really important. Do whatever you need to do to make that a reality for yourself, even if it means sacrificing the external success markers of high income, senior position, etc.

We have a high sense of moral justice and will often use that in our working lives. We stand up for others (for example in bullying situations), often to the point that we are exhausted as we become a magnet for strife and discord. One of my clients took on a nursing supervisory role and found all the student nurses were coming to him to air their grievances and discuss their problems and he would go home after a shift feeling totally exhausted. They had offloaded their problems, but he had taken them into his body. He had to leave that job because it was too overwhelming to continue.

---

[i] The word vocation comes from the Latin vocare and means calling.

In terms of general self-care, we need to have emotionally nourishing situations in which to flourish so having good self-care routines is vital. This doesn't mean just pampering yourself from time to time (that is good though!), it means making time for beauty and pleasure in your daily routines (walks in nature, and in creative environments), time out of over-stimulation and speaking up for our truth without apology. Having an authentic expression in our daily lives isn't an optional extra it's essential[i].

Because we flourish in natural environments, we often find unwinding easiest when walking in woods, or on the beach, gardening or fishing. Many sensitives even make a living out of their love of animals or nature becoming outdoor rangers, forest schoolteachers, dog walkers, etc. The quality of our daily lives becomes very much more enhanced that way. Don't forget we benefit more from positive experiences – so with the right nurturance we fly!

---

[i] I would say everyone (whether sensitive or not) should have this, but it's especially important for sensitives.

Harnessing the Strengths of High Sensitivity:

Make sure that you choose activities that highlight the strengths and advantages that come with high sensitivity, such as creativity, intuition, deep processing, and attention to detail. Stop forcing yourself into the wrong sized life and be proud of your unique gifts. Know that more joy is possible, but it has to start with you choosing a life that fits you.

Our final chapter examines this in more detail.

## CHAPTER SEVEN – HOW TO THRIVE WITH A SENSE OF BELONGING

So, we've examined both the neurological basis and the experience of being highly sensitive – both positive and negative. We've seen that it is often misdiagnosed by traditional medicine which focusses on the symptoms (caused by the sensitivity interacting with trauma) – with little result. Even holistic /alternative practitioners may miss this[i] with a lot of tests that diagnose nutritional deficiencies, etc. but ignore the underlying cause.

Let's now look at what we can do to boost our experience of life as highly sensitive people. Remember that everyone's experience as an HSP is unique, so it's important to explore and experiment with different strategies to discover what works best for you.

---

[i] As a practitioner you should take a detailed history but add a few key questions from the HSP quiz and maybe adding some of your own like "when attending events do you prefer to take your own car so you can leave when you want?". A checklist for sensitive patients so they are not mislabeled or medicated is vital.

# Thriving in a Non-sensitive World:

We need to address the challenges of navigating a world that may not always understand or accommodate high sensitivity, and in this chapter, I want to include tips for advocating for oneself, finding supportive communities, and embracing one's unique traits.

## SPS is Your Superpower

In order to begin I want to borrow a little from Elaine Eron's concept of 'Five to Thrive' and then augment it further with my own experience and those of my clients.

Five to Thrive:

1. Understand the trait is real.

2. Design a life that is compatible.

3. Reframe the past in light of that understanding.

4. Heal from past trauma.

5. Know and be supported by other sensitive people.

1 Understanding the trait is real.

This is an important first step. If you are in any doubt, then you will be in denial of your authentic self and battling to survive in a world that doesn't support you. If you are not able to at least advocate for your needs your body will find a way to force you! The body (and the brain it connects with) is a source of highly intelligent information not just a physical lump of matter. It always has the best intentions for you. Seeing that neuroscience now supports a differential susceptibility to life events is key to being at peace with yourself for being just the way you are.

2 Designing a life that is compatible.

means refusing to squeeze yourself into situations and a life that makes you tense and limits you. We will delve into this in more detail in this chapter but the essence of this is making a *life that fits you* and not the other way round. Little changes have big results.

3 Reframe the past in the light of that understanding.

Seeing that it wasn't YOU that was wrong or inadequate but the type of support you got takes away much of the shame and bewilderment that having high sensitivity as a child creates. It enables a reframing of your past experience with compassion for what you experienced as *understandable* rather than as something you created somehow through being 'wrong' (more shame).

Shame lives on in you as a shadow of negativity about who you are and will undermine most of your attempts to heal yourself. It is vital to come into a compassionate relationship with yourself as this helps not only to change your mental state but also your body's responses. Compassion is the antidote to shame. It neither seeks to minimise the pain you went through or live in victimhood but acknowledges the truth of your experience so that you can release it and let it go.

4 Heal from past trauma.

Linked to the previous statement, dealing with unhealed trauma is vital. You cannot change what happened to you, but you can change your response to what happened and thus your experience of life now. Sadly, the scripts of the past only get more fixed the longer we carry on repeating them and in order to truly get free of it we need to release the trauma through the body's responses.[i]

Don't forget that past trauma adds to the sensitive brain's already highly altered perceptions and creates a greater stress response so it's vital to release unhealed wounds from the past if you truly want to thrive.

---

[i] And that's not as painful or difficult as it might sound. Sometimes all that's needed is to let the body shake or allow a sensation to pass through when recalling the past experience. Other times it's best to deal with individual instances that overwhelmed you. But always in the company of a safe person, preferably therapist.

5 Know and be supported by other sensitive people.

It is such a validating experience to be understood by people who feel about the world the way you do. Creating a community therefore, or at least having one or two highly sensitive friends can change your experience of yourself and help to build self-esteem and resilience. Knowing you're not alone in your sensitivity will banish feelings of shame and inadequacy as you will feel validated.

## From Survival to Thrival

Thriving as a highly sensitive person involves embracing your sensitivity, understanding your unique needs and implementing self-care practices that support your well-being.

I'd like to finish the book with some more detailed perspectives to help you thrive as a highly sensitive person, using examples:

The first step is, of course, about becoming aware of your sensitivity.

Take the time to understand and accept your sensitivity as a natural part of who you are. Recognize your specific triggers, emotions, and boundaries. Self-awareness helps you navigate your experiences more effectively. Prioritise yourself as someone who matters!

A great tip here is to allow yourself to listen to your body's messages without fear or self-criticism. 80% of our information in our brain comes from our body via the **vagus nerve** and most of us are completely disconnected from the body's messages. Take time to become aware of them and spend time with yourself and your past history if that is relevant.

If you find that too triggering seek help with a qualified practitioner who can help stabilise your nervous system in order for you to be able to listen without fear. There are also great self-help stabilization methods like tapping (EFT), havening and TRE (trauma release exercises). But if you are aware you have a traumatic history, I recommend working with someone as the triggering can be too great on your own.

Case Study - Carla

Carla had never acknowledged her sensitivity until I did a presentation on it which she watched. She said it was without doubt the most important talk she had ever heard. It knocked her completely sideways for several days as she suddenly realised how much she had ignored her needs for decades. She recalled as a teenager having a much greater awareness of her difference and actually celebrating that by being a 'goth'. But as her twenties approached, she knuckled down to get a job and become more 'normal'. She started to forget who she was as there was no reflection of that reality in her life, so she subsumed it to her great detriment.

It was only after her body effectively collapsed in her 40's that she was forced to stop and re-evaluate her pushing through coping strategy and see how that had ignored her sensitivity to environment. She now recognises the importance of not forcing yourself into situations that do not reflect who you are and is taking the first steps to creating a life that fits her and not a life she has to squeezer herself into. Although this is going to take time as she has to find a new role, she is feeling confident at last that she's never going back to the old ways.

SELF-CARE:

Prioritize self-care activities that help you recharge and maintain emotional balance. This may include creating quiet and peaceful environments, engaging in activities that bring you joy and relaxation, practicing mindfulness or meditation, yoga or tai chi, or simply getting enough restful sleep, and eating nutritious meals. If you find yourself bingeing or scrolling on your device instead of relaxing, then you may have an issue with anxiety.

Anxiety will over-rule your natural propensity to self-care as it will tell you:

- There isn't enough time (there is always time if you prioritise yourself).

- You don't deserve it! (Another shame story).

- It's selfish (which is all about messages you received as a child and totally untrue). Self-care is a form of self-love and that is totally nurturing and life-affirming.

## Case Study- Elena

Elena had stopped all self-care activities except the very basic ones (and even those like washing her hair had become occasional). It was not just the effort that stopped her, it was the will to see herself as valid or deserving. Sadly, her parents had managed to communicate the message that she was only worthy if she was achieving goals or winning awards, as she had done at school. Now as an adult, she felt useless, and life had become devoid of meaning. This had happened so gradually that she'd hardly noticed the gradual chipping away of joy. As she had focused more on her job than on her wellbeing, stress began to take its toll.

In order to reverse this gradual loss of self-care (which comes from lack of self-esteem), we had to show her that her experience of herself was incomplete and distorted. That she possessed amazing creativity that was calling out to be channeled. I asked her to begin drawing and painting again (a favourite activity as a child). It began to liberate her from needing to be productive in order to feel valid.

As she started to express her pent-up emotions from years of repression, she saw the beauty of her abilities and that it was not her that was wrong but her environment. Gradually a respect and love for herself returned and she took pride in self-care activities which have become part of her lived experience of herself. No longer the outsider looking in, she belongs to herself and to her life.

BOUNDARIES:

Establish and communicate your boundaries clearly with others. Learn to say no when necessary and advocate for yourself. Setting boundaries helps you manage your energy levels and protect yourself from overwhelm, and it may be as simple as learning to stop agreeing with everyone and decide for yourself what you want.

# Case study – Carmel

Carmel grew up believing she had to be a good girl to avoid causing a problem for her parents, particularly her mother who was loving but temperamental. Any time she tried to communicate her need for space or time to process, both parents would squash that and tell her to 'buck up' and get on with things. They were both very hard working so had little time for her 'whingeing' as they called it. She learned to be very compliant and ignore her needs completely.

If offered a choice she would say – 'I don't mind, you decide', and then feel secretly resentful when the choice was not one she wanted. She buried that anger for years and it only came out when in her relationship her partner wanted to have an open relationship and she reluctantly agreed even though it was contrary to her values of monogamy, and she felt very belittled. Eventually after attending a yoga retreat for women, she felt empowered to say 'no' and end the relationship. Although very hard as she loved him, his decisions were no longer in accordance with what she knew she wanted and her values. As a sensitive person she discovered she could not tolerate a life where her values were ignored or attacked.

She spent a couple of years alone, gathering herself before meeting someone who wanted to commit to her and is now exploring new boundaries that state clearly what her needs are.

Not everyone has to do what Carmel did and many relationships can change and adapt to new boundaries, indeed may thrive because finally your partner has a clearer idea of what you need. Learning to say 'no' to what no longer serves you allows you to say 'yes' to the things that make your life worth living. Many people end up burnt out and compromised from this lack of boundary making and it's a very important skill to learn. Notice if you say 'sorry' all the time - make a pact with yourself you will only apologise for things that require it.

Never apologise for being you, be clear and you will be rewarded in ways you never imagined possible.

EMOTIONAL REGULATION:

Develop techniques to regulate your emotions effectively. This might include deep breathing exercises, journaling, talking to a trusted friend or therapist, or engaging in creative outlets such as art, music, or writing. Learning self-help techniques that are body-based rather than cognitive makes this much more powerful. Remember it is the emotional brain that's really in charge and its connections with your body via the autonomic nervous system are what is driving this dysregulation.

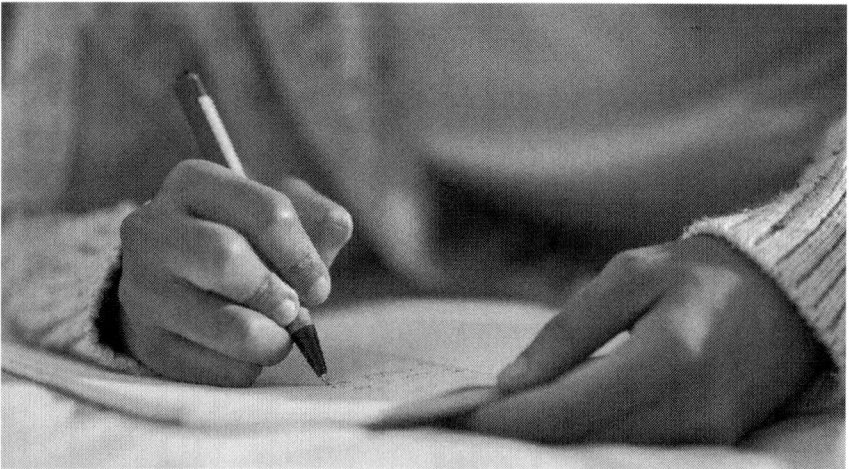

# Case Study – Brian

Brian had accepted himself as 'faulty' - somehow too sensitive for the world. He saw it as a total negative, not helped by the fact his children would sometimes mock him for it. He found travel very stressful – the London underground was impossible due to his agoraphobia and planes were a battle against panic. Even when travelling by car he would imagine all the worst-case scenarios before any trip. His teenage kids found him difficult to understand although his son shared some of his sensitivity, he was in denial, so it caused a lot of tension in the family.

His wife however recognised that maybe he needed to work on some of the negative traumas that were underlying his reactions so that his life could become less limited and his nervous system more regulated, whilst understanding that he was a sensitive man (that's what she loved about him after all). Separating out the trauma reaction from the underlying sensitivity was important. It's ok to be sensitive but it shouldn't be life limiting.

Once he'd worked on the repressed grief of losing his father to dementia, Brian's agoraphobia began to reduce. He found he could travel as long as he created space for his emotions and calmed his fears with self-regulation techniques. I taught him havening whilst making certain affirmations to yourself like "I am here, I am safe, all is well" to rebalance the nervous system. He began to pay attention to his fear as a message rather than an instruction.

When I showed him that many panic reactions have suppressed emotional memories at their core, we could explore those with EMDR and he could resolve them as over. Now he journals regularly whenever he notices something isn't quite right and leans into the feeling instead of trying to push it away. His children are now onboard and even asking him what he does to deal with anxiety! Although he's not ever going to be 'un-sensitive', he now has developed skills to deal with it so that he is not so limited.

STRESS MANAGEMENT:

Find healthy and effective ways to manage stress. This could involve engaging in regular exercise, practicing relaxation techniques, exploring stress-reducing hobbies, or incorporating mindfulness practices into your daily routine. You can also take flower essences as a natural, gentle alternative to nutritional stress busting supplements. Start with Rescue Remedy (a very basic essence that should be in every sensitive's handbag/ backpack. Great for shocks and untoward experiences).

If one of your high values is moral justice (which is often the case for many sensitives), and you find yourself often speaking up for others, then learn to let go of the need to help *everyone*. It's not always possible or desirable to push yourself into situations where you are ignoring your own needs to try to solve the needs of others. This is like trying to save a drowning person and then drowning yourself. It serves no useful purpose.

# Case Study - Paul

Paul was a senior nurse trainer in a large hospital trust. He was drawn to the nursing profession out of love for helping others, but he found the environment much more cut and thrust than he was expecting. Many of the more junior nurses came to him with their management problems and he felt duty-bound to sort them out. He would often do an extra hour or two after his shift making phonecalls and talking to colleagues. He would come home exhausted, and it was beginning to take a toll on his marriage. His sleep was also affected as the issues would go round and round in his head at night too. When I saw him, he looked dreadful, and I asked him - what are you taking on that you need to let go of? We saw that his need to help others had got out of balance and his stress levels were through the roof.

I made no judgements about the nature of the job, although I did ask why he needed to take extra shifts when he was officially in semi-retirement. I simply showed him stress management techniques of havening and tapping (EFT), which I find very useful with clients as it rebalances their vagus nerve (which helps to promote a relaxation response). However, when I checked in with him a couple of months later, he had given in his notice as he realised that he was punishing himself for not being fully productive, as retirement had always seemed like a dead end for him. Now he was looking forward to his retirement by going on trips with his wife and taking up running in the park at weekends.

In many ways this case study could also sit in the heading 'Boundaries' because it was learning to say 'no' to the extra work that was being piled onto him that enabled him to make a better decision that worked for him Not everyone is lucky enough to be able to leave their job and still have a good income but there are always ways and means when you get out of the stress cycle.

## Case Study 2 – Andrea

Andrea also worked in the health sector as a social support worker. Driven very much like Brian to help others but she'd found the work increasingly stressful and had been laid off on sick leave since being diagnosed with chronic fatigue syndrome in her late 40's. although her employers were sympathetic, they were about to cut her sick pay to half pay and she was both terrified of having no income and also of having to go back to work and all the stress. She was in a terrible 'double bind' that no amount of thinking seemed to alleviate. The more she worried, the worse her symptoms got.

When we began our work together, my aim was to help her get a new perspective on her situation – was there another way she and her family could cut cost so that going back to work was not necessary? She and her husband decided to downsize their house so that they could live on his income, and she would take early retirement. Although initially she had a lot of shame around leaving (she is a sensitive after all!), she came to realise that when she analysed the work situation, she saw that the best 'stress management' technique for her was to accept that the work situation no longer worked for her. And by accepting that, she came to see that other possibilities would arise. She is now considering dog walking as a part-time self-employment to bring in some cash as she's always loved animals.

HEALTHY RELATIONSHIPS:

Surround yourself with understanding and supportive individuals who appreciate your sensitivity. Cultivate relationships that uplift and respect your unique needs. Seek out like-minded communities or support groups where you can connect with others who share similar experiences. Make that a priority!

Relationships can be both the greatest and the most challenging aspect of a sensitive person's life. Because we take them so seriously it is hard for us when they have difficulties or end. Our ability to process is somewhat hampered by our enhanced empathy which means we are feeling not only our own feelings but those of the other to whom we are attached so disentangling that can be very tricky. But we make great friends and partners when our sensitivity is supported so finding relaxing nurturing relationships is one of the main ways in which we can self-care.

This may entail ending ones that no longer support us in ways we need – and this is hard for us to do as we feel like we are betraying a trust somehow when we put our own needs first.

Finding ones that nurture us is perhaps a lifelong quest which becomes easier the better you know yourself and your emotional needs and values. But pay attention to them and they will sustain.

When we think of healthy relationships, we often ignore our animal friends. But for sensitives animals are a great companion and may actually be just what we need to help put a spring in our step again. Although some people are daunted by the responsibility, you don't always need to take on a pet yourself but could share ownership responsibilities with someone, perhaps house or pet-sitting as a business or joining a group of dog walkers, volunteering at your local horse stables for instance.

## Case Study - Malvi

Malvi found herself struggling with relationships. They would always start well with a feeling that she was finally going to be loved and taken care of, but as soon as she got close to someone, she would start to pull away. Intimacy would trigger her limbic brain as a threat – without safety closeness is seen as immobility without escape! So, she would find herself closing down and pushing the person away. She lived with the guilt of that and decided to stop having relationships as they were too painful when they ended.

When we examined Malvi's deep wounds having never had the emotional support she needed as a child (and indeed being the emotional buffer for her family!), we saw that in order to survive she'd had to close down her attachment system. This only gets triggered when you get really close to someone, so it didn't stop her wanting closeness or attempting to find it, it just hijacked her whenever her feelings for someone deepened.

By helping her to heal the hurt of the past, we were able to allow her body's set point for stress to lower so that she could tolerate more uncertainty or intimacy without shutting down. She has begun to practice opening up a little with her family and is hopeful that she will once again be able to tolerate the sometimes painful emotions that being misunderstood or having to compromise in love a relationship brings.

I always suggest starting with the easy wins first which builds emotional resilience. Then, as you gain more emotional mastery, you can again take the risk of being loved without feeling so overwhelmed. This allows your emotional brain to be fully integrated with your thinking brain (which oversees all activities like a CEO). It's like you get internal approval for a new response.

TIME ALONE:

Allow yourself regular periods of solitude and reflection. Highly sensitive individuals often benefit from time alone to recharge and process their experiences without external stimulation. This could be yoga, meditation, sewing or crafting, going fishing, walking, gardening, etc. Whatever allows you to forget time and play a little bit, is going to help your subconscious brain to assimilate (digest) its experience without going into overwhelm. Being active is just as good as resting because it uses procedural memory. You want to get out of thinking for a while and into feeling.

## Case Study – Rona

Rona never gave herself a minute to reflect or be alone, she was always on the go. If she stopped, the painful anxiety would well up and she feared she would collapse, so she kept going well past the time when she needed rest. Sometimes she would stay up til the early hours scrolling and chatting with people on the internet – she recognised it was out of control, but she seemed powerless to stop the urge. She needed others to keep her from looking inside.

When we examined where this was coming from there was a deep belief that if she stopped, she would be overcome with grief and she couldn't allow that. It felt like she had to get 'one step ahead of the devil stalking me'. But the devil was actually her unprocessed feelings and can't be avoided without severe consequences for her health. She'd been finding less and less energy and it took her days to recover whenever she had a 'crash'. Working was impossible and she was living on benefits with multiple symptoms (POTS, CFS/ME*, Lyme and vertigo).

Her thinking brain was over-ruling her emotional brain and she was in thrall to her addiction. We needed to bring back her emotional expression and allow her to be heard, time to herself and for her to hear her own pain without fear. As she allowed herself to be witnessed her urges got less intense and she was able to find alternative ways to calm herself. Although she is not yet back to working, there is the possibility of volunteering locally which she is contemplating as she would like to feel like she is contributing again. Small steps make big changes possible.

## Case Study 2 – William

William worked in a busy government department office. He was their 'go-to' person for all queries and issues as he was so competent and good at his job. He'd worked his way to a fairly senior position and was increasing feeling like his time was no longer his own. He worked longer and longer hours, often working on weekends to catch up and his wife was beginning to complain that it was affecting their relationship. But he felt like he was on a treadmill that he couldn't get off of. If he let people down, who would he be? He had always prided himself on his reliability.

However, his body had other ideas. On their summer vacation, he suddenly found himself unable to interact socially with friends, and things became very intensely uncomfortable suddenly and he felt dizzy and anxious. To his immense shame, he and his wife had to come home early, and he went straight to bed. He realised suddenly that there was no possibility of going back to work the next week and he was signed off for 4 weeks.

His wife, having recognised this was quite serious contacted me and asked if I would talk to him. Luckily William was very open to being helped and we started work on some of the grief that he'd not processed and how he had buried that in overwork and lack of alone time. When finally, he was well enough to return to work, he went back part-time so that he could pursue his love of the outdoors a volunteer ranger. This gave him time to process his feelings while doing practical tasks that gave his thinking brain a rest.

When we ignore our need for rest and alone time, our worries do not go away, they bury themselves in our body which bears the burden. Eventually this may cause disease and even physical symptoms. Make sure you take time out to process – remember you need more time and space than most people.

MINDFUL AND HARMONIOUS ENVIRONMENTS:

Create an environment at home that promotes calmness and reduces sensory overload. Consider factors such as lighting, noise levels, and organization to create a space where you feel comfortable and at ease. It could be a corner of the living area or bedroom that's cosy with cushions and a beautiful lamp or picture, it could be a space in the garden or outdoor space with a hammock or chair with a view. Whatever it is, consider how you feel in that space and make sure it's harmonious. Sensitive people really respond to harmony.

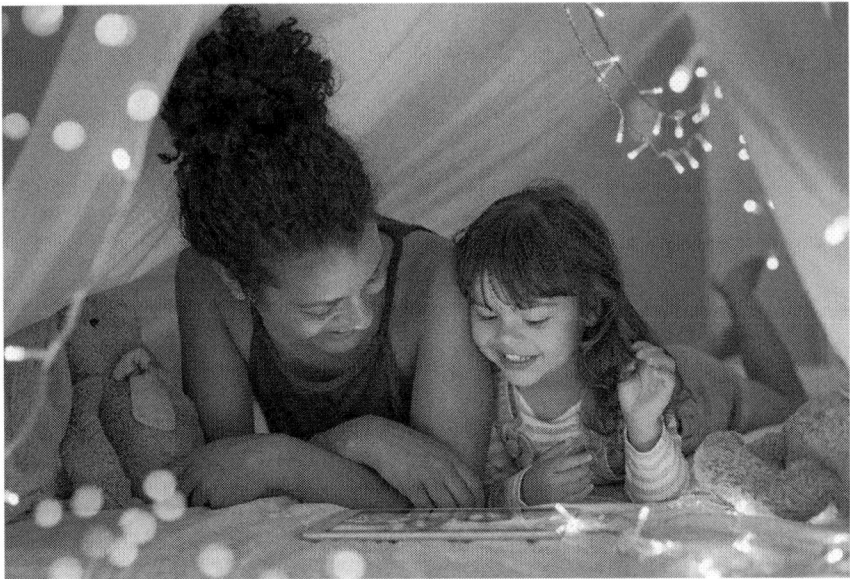

Where you work and play *matters* and they should be very distinct spaces. Choose the colours wisely because your nervous system appreciates harmony and will notice when things are clashing.

You can experiment a little with colour – see what moods they create in you. For my work environment writing this, I am in a pale duck-egg blue room with soft grey curtains. The desk is oak along with the rest of the furniture, so that there is contrasting colour and warmth. There is an picture in front of me by the author of the Moomin stories, Tove Jansson who was a wonderful illustrator. It never fails to inspire me.

You will undoubtedly have your own favourite colours and they will vary depending on the natural light present in the room. Our nervous systems like natural light so have some semi-transparent voile at the window which allows a soft light to penetrate over the desk. If you work from home like I do, make sure your files are stacked on a shelf rather than overflowing onto the desk (as used to be the case!). You will feel more at peace working in a space that is organised.

In other rooms, with different functions, you may need something stronger or more dramatic. Lighting is really key – fairy lights or soft lighting add a cosy, inviting touch in the living room – whatever the time of year!

For work areas get yourself a full-spectrum light which has all the frequencies of natural daylight. Blue tinged LED lights are deadening not only to the atmosphere but to your soul[i]. You may choose them for efficiency and cost savings but make sure you choose the soft white version.

---

[i] Ever wondered why some supermarkets or public toilets feel so depressing? It's the lighting and space layout – and we sensitives really notice this subliminally.

## Case Study – Michelle

Michelle works from home but so her 'office' is the kitchen table or wherever she happens to be. This means that her living space is a multi-tasking, somewhat disordered environment that has to be periodically cleared away to make room for other activities. When I asked her what was the one thing she most craved it was a harmonious environment. But she hadn't made the connection that her failure to create a proper space for work away from her family space was causing her body stress.

So, she determined to not only clear a junk room to make space for a desk with some gorgeous prints that she could look at while working, but she also created a meditation corner in the living area with a lamp and some cushions where she could just chill out away from the distractions of TV, or phone. When she made space for herself like this, her body felt loved and supported as well as her mind having more space for creativity and flow.

Now Michelle finds that she isn't in such a rush to get things done as they have to be cleared away and she can get up and stretch and walk maybe between tasks to allow her body to move, rather than constantly feeling under pressure. She even sets a timer on her phone to remind her to get up from time to time. Movement is so key for the body to function well!

Now not everyone has the luxury of a spare room but there is always a way to create a corner somewhere that feels good. Small changes create big results. Remember harmony is sensory – and you can achieve it in simple ways via sight, sound and touch. A cosy cushion or blanket to stroke, (or even resident pet!), sends a message to your brain that you are safe[i].

---

[i] Hence why cats, dogs and horses are often recommend for calming the nervous systems of neurodiverse children and adults.

POSITIVE MINDSET:

Foster a positive and compassionate mindset towards yourself. Practice self-acceptance, self-compassion, and gratitude. Focus on your strengths and embrace the gifts that come with sensitivity, such as heightened empathy and creativity, embrace your oddness/difference from others. Connect with people, animals and nature to bring back the joy!

This one sounds obvious doesn't it – think positively and be kind to yourself! But it's far more than that. Positivity for a start has to be genuine. If you're just plastering over the cracks by answering a 'how are you?' with 'fine, thanks' yet secretly you're sad and angry, that is not self-compassionate. Being falsely positive is a major issue for many of the clients I work with as they look ok, but inside they feel terrible. Having a dysregulated nervous system doesn't necessarily look obvious – you're not limping or shaking, but you feel terrible inside.

That's not to say we dwell in victimhood or burden everyone with our woes, but we need to at the very least be honest with ourselves about how we're feeling in order to process those emotions. In other words, we need to be able to allow the emotion to be metabolised and thus our body can move on. Otherwise, the emotions sit in the body causing mayhem.

Studies have shown that different emotions have different outcomes in the body. I have found that buried anger tends to go to the heart or stomach and buried guilt is in the back. But Louise Hay mapped these pain patterns more accurately in her book 'Heal your Life' -see Resources at end.

You may also wish to consider coming off social media or at the very least restricting its use. It is not good being bathed in all that comparison to everyone else all of the time and it actually drives anxiety. Matt Haig writes about this in his book 'Notes on a Nervous Planet' as a time of distraction. Have real conversations with real people instead.

## Case Study – Michael

Michael has a nagging pain in his back that he had on and off for ten years. It had caused him to leave his previous office job as sitting for too long caused the pain to get worse. He was convinced he needed a job where he could move more and took a lower grade job as a manager in a store where at least he could have a variety of tasks and get to be upright for much of the day. But the pain never went away completely, and he wondered if there might be an emotional root cause.

We looked at his history and found that there had been an event in his childhood which had never left him. Taking on the responsibility for his mother when his father left home suddenly and feeling his mother's anguish. Realizing he was now the 'man of the house' he took a child's view of life into his adulthood and even when minor things triggered him, he would feel a deep sense of responsibility for any and all difficult events in his life and then guilt when he wasn't able to accomplish solving them all.

By helping him to acknowledge the unhealed guilt inside him, his body was able to relax and let go and the back pain disappeared. It still occasionally returns but Michael now takes that as a warning sign that he is taking on too much again and uses this knowledge to get help or support.

SEEK SUPPORT:

If needed, seek support from therapists, counselors, or coaches who specialize in working with highly sensitive individuals. They can provide guidance and tools tailored to your specific needs. If you get a bad feeling working with someone, trust that they're probably not for you. The interpersonal connection is way more important than the tools or type of therapy they offer (though I would say somatic or body-based work is better than cognitive for the sorts of issues discussed here).

Remember there is no shame in asking for help – calming your nervous system requires a safe other nervous system to borrow from! That's why we struggle to fix this ourselves. Join support groups online or preferably in person if you would like more support. I run a monthly **Community Session** (see Resources).

Be patient with yourself and celebrate the progress you make along the way. However, it's not necessary to jettison everything all at once, you can develop your exit plan gradually. Learning to trust that your body recognises this problem and has been trying to tell you for years is an important revelation. Knowing that you can communicate back is powerful. Reassure your body which will inform your mind that all is well.

And finally...

Play with other modes of expression e.g., art – drawing/painting, pottery, crafting, etc., feel how it would be to enjoy your job that much... Practicing feeling good, even if it isn't your everyday experience allows your subconscious mind to experience joy.

Mind the gap between stimulus and response – allow a new neurological pathway to open up by deliberately pausing between something that causes you to feel emotionally triggered and your habitual response means you can change your response to one that is more in keeping with your needs. Learning to say 'I don't know, I'll get back to you' or 'let me think about that' is a good stalling phrase while you get your emotional house in order.

This allows you to foster better and more authentic relationships where you are not following an old script – what Dr Joe Dispenza calls 'the habit of being you'. Get together with other HSPs or empaths so that you can be truly understood and felt. Allow yourself to be felt and if that is alien to you, tell yourself that you are learning to accept yourself and be accepted. It's a process not a destination. Let yourself be guided perhaps by more seasoned empaths to teach the beginners. I love the work of Joan Rosenberg and Judith Orwell (see Resources) which helps us to accept all our emotions and not be afraid of their expression – however strong they feel.

Encouraging self-acceptance, building resilience, and fostering a positive mindset to embrace and thrive as a highly sensitive individual requires an evolution of body and mind. It is not about pushing through or 'fixing the problem' (both stressful experiences for the body).

If you are suffering any long-term chronic condition you may need to do more guided work with a therapist to truly break the old patterns. We are often blind to ourselves and particularly our unconscious process. See the Chrysalis Effect Program also my Thrive and Emotional AUDIT courses (see **my website** in Resources for details).

- Learn what your values are and live by them[i].
- Learn to trust your body and your life.

That is where safety lies.

---

[i] You can do the values exercise available on my website and elsewhere.

# APPENDIX 1 – FUN HSP QUIZ
My Highly Sensitive Questions (in addition to Elaine Aron's)

- Do you find loud noisy reverberating rooms difficult to concentrate in? e.g., wood paneled flooring in restaurants? Or having builders in your home or next door that you can't switch off from?
- Do you find it difficult to concentrate on the phone if someone else is talking to you at the same time?
- Do you find it hard to ignore a stone in your shoe, a scratchy label in your clothes or something in your eye i.e., you HAVE to stop and sort it out immediately!
- Do sirens or loud noises immediately cause a nervous system response i.e., your heart speeds up or there is a knot in your stomach.
- Does the sound of a dog barking or baby crying make you uneasy – especially if it sounds like it is anxious or upset?
- Do you avoid watching images on the TV of violence, disaster, suffering because you can't sleep afterwards?
- Do you find yourself rejecting invitations whereby you have no control about when to leave and prefer to take your own transport?
- Does the suffering of other people feel like it's in your own body? Especially people you are emotionally close to?
- Do you find yourself lost in imagining conversations or alternative endings to experiences you've had or witnessed and it's difficult to let it go?
- Do arguments and conflicts wound you deeply?

# APPENDIX 2 -SELF-CARE EMERGENCY KIT

## Self-Care and Well-being Techniques:

We have seen that self-care is often the first thing to be dropped when people are suffering overwhelm. Having an emergency self-care practice is vital for those unexpected moments where something happens that we cannot control. What do I suggest (and use myself).

- Bach Flower Essence Rescue Remedy – have some in your bag ready for emergencies. Flower essences are extremely gentle on your nervous system and are very subtle ways to stabilise your nervous system.
- Take yourself to the bathroom/restroom and practice havening. See my video online here.
- Get support for how you're feeling, ask for a hug. Do NOT suffer alone if you can at all help it.
- When you are able you will need to find a way of processing what's happened. Tapping, shaking (TRE technique), journalling or doing something manual that takes up your brain's attention and leaves you less time to over-think. Gardening, walking, drawing, painting and crafts all come in that category. Sometimes it's better to do this in company so that you can talk about things if you need to. But whatever you do, make sure you give yourself time to process. See the resources at the end for ideas of tapping videos or my youtube channel for further information.

## Resources

## Books

Elaine N. Aron, *The Highly Sensitive Person*. A fantastic book written in easy-to-understand language about how hypersensitivity affects people throughout life. Although not explicitly a book about trauma, it covers the same ground.

Brené Brown, Daring Greatly: How the Courage to Be Vulnerable Transforms the Way We Live, Love, Parent, and Lead. About the way shame invades our culture and what makes you shame resilient.

Bessel Van der Kolk, *The Body Keeps the Score*. With a long career in trauma rehabilitation and treatment, this is the absolute bible for trauma treatment.

Peter Levine, *Healing Trauma* and *Chasing the Tiger*. Both classics show how an uncompleted freeze response may lie behind the chronic symptoms of trauma.

Bruce Lipton, *The Biology of Belief*. One of the first books to explain epigenetics i.e., the effect of the environment on the genetic expression of DNA. A must read.

Gabor Mate, *The Myth of Normal*. How our culture of perfectionism and toxicity takes its toll.

Judith Orloff, *The Empaths Survival Guide*. Tools for a great life.

Robert Scaer, *The Body Bears the Burden*. Another really great book which looks in detail at the neurobiology of trauma and how it translates into damage to brain and body.

Francine Shapiro, *Getting Past your Past*. A book on EMDR technique for the layperson.

Pete Walker, The Tao of Fully Feeling and Complex PTSD

## Websites

Alchemy Therapies (my therapy website)

**https://alchemytherapies.co.uk**

See also my YouTube channel @PatriciaWorbyPhD and my interview with a senior lawyer on maintaining emotional equilibrium at work. **https://youtu.be/E5TYi9dEBEU**

And my how to do tapping/havening video -

**https://youtu.be/PFr2eDcYE-I**

Michael Ploess of QMC, London Sensitivity Research website with incredible resources in lay person language. **https://sensitivityresearch.com/**

http://www.alchemytherapies.co.uk – my therapy website.

Joan Rosenberg – Emotional Mastery TED talk - **https://www.youtube.com/watch?v=EKy19WzkPxE**

The Tapping Solution – great site for tapping ideas and videos **https://www.thetappingsolution.com/**

## Courses

**Thrive** is my introductory Mind and Body connection course.

The **Emotional AUDIT** is a more advanced understanding which is self-led or occasionally, I run them as group courses. See my website for details. https://www.alchemytherapies.co.uk/challenge-page/myea-evergreen

For more on trauma see my Thinkific Course page. **https://dr-patricia-worby-alchemy-training.thinkific.com/courses**

# GLOSSARY OF TECHNICAL TERMS

(*First mentions in the text are in bold*).

**Amygdala** - almond-shaped threat-sensor of the brain's limbic system.

**Anabolic -** a building/repair physiological state induced by rest and relaxation (compared with catabolic)

**Autonomic nervous system (ANS)** - part of the nervous system responsible for automatic actions like breathing, heart rate, etc. Happens without conscious control.

**Anterior cingulate cortex (ACC)** - the filtering system of the brain.

**Biomedical model** – the belief in modern medicine that all disease originates in the organ of its presentation. Compare biopsychosocial.

**Biopsychosocial** – a model of health which accounts for the biological, psychological processes interacting with the social environment.

**Catabolic** – a breakdown physiological state – can be induced by stress.

**Catastrophising** - act of constructing a worst-case scenario from past experience, one of the many cognitive distortions we make routinely.

**Central nervous system (CNS)** – the brain and spinal cord. With the peripheral nervous system allows our interaction with the sensory world.

**Complex Emotions** – the emotions like abandonment, betrayal and humiliation which particularly embed themselves as they have a strong meaning overlay.

**Dopaminergic response/ reward system** – the system in the brain that motivates us to seek gratification and uses the neurotransmitter dopamine.

**Epigenetics -** the environmental influences that turn on or off genetic expression. Can be dietary, exercise or beliefs – see biopsychosocial model.

**Emotional resilience** – ability to respond appropriately to stresses without being overwhelmed by your feelings.

**Genetic determinism -** the belief, widely promulgated in the media that we are the random result of genes – good or bad. See Epigenetics

**Hippocampus** - part of the limbic system that date-stamps events and stores them as memories in the past.

**Hyper-vigilance** – the propensity to focus on potential threat at the expense of safety so that we are always on alert.

**Hypothalamus- Pituitary - Adrenal system (HPA) axis** - interconnected, three-part system of brain and endocrine organs that communicates and activates the stress response.

**Limbic System** -the mammalian or 'emotional brain 'consisting of: thalamus (relay station), hypothalamus (threat evaluator), hippocampus (date stamp and our normal memory processing centre), and the amygdala, the brain's fire alarm/smoke detector.

**Neurodiversity** - the term given to the range of nervous system function and behavioural traits, regarded as part of normal variation in the human population - adaptations along a spectrum of responses.

**Neuroplasticity -** environmental brain adaptations building new nerve connections to make more energy efficient and automatic processes.

**Psychosensory therapy** - therapy that uses sensation (touch, vision, hearing, etc.) to help connect with the limbic system of the brain and resolve stuck emotions. Sometimes also called energy psychology.

**Rumination** – the overthinking strategy that many HSPs adopt in the hope it will avoid the problem. But all it does is create more stress.

**Sensory processing sensitivity** (**SPS**) - the term given to the way the brains 14 of Highly Sensitive people perceive and process differently to neurotypical people.

**Sensory Processing Disorder (SPD)**- distinct developmental condition which may result from birth or early life trauma. Has a checklist of symptoms which has a lot of overlap with other neurodevelopmental disorders in that it shares autonomic dysregulation with them as its baseline.

**Somatisation** - feeling emotions through the body rather than as consciously perceived feelings.

**Sympathetic dominance** - where the fight and flight mechanism of the autonomic nervous system becomes perpetually triggered and the person feels anxious, activated and in pain.

**Toxic stress** - the kind of stress that overwhelms our nervous system's capacity to cope.  As compared to normal or motivational stress (eustress). Very linked to childhood trauma and the beliefs that engenders.

This Book also available as an Audiobook (on amazon and Audible) plus Other Books You'll Love:

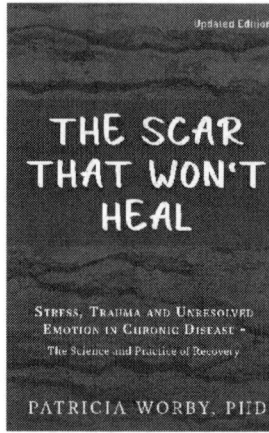

Updated Edition

## THE SCAR THAT WON'T HEAL

STRESS, TRAUMA AND UNRESOLVED
EMOTION IN CHRONIC DISEASE -
The Science and Practice of Recovery

PATRICIA WORBY, PHD

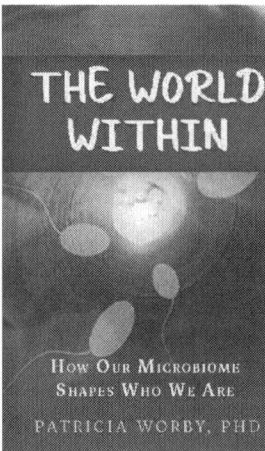

## THE WORLD WITHIN

HOW OUR MICROBIOME
SHAPES WHO WE ARE

PATRICIA WORBY, PHD

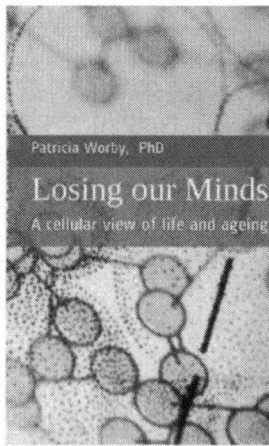

Patricia Worby, PhD

Losing our Minds

A cellular view of life and ageing

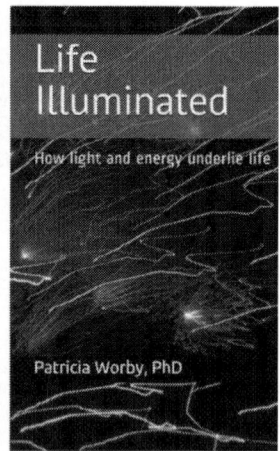

## Life Illuminated

How light and energy underlie life

Patricia Worby, PhD

See my Author page here (**US**) or (**UK**)

*Just for You!*

A Special Gift for my Readers:

Hidden Trauma – A Guide to Healing the Past (and why you need to)
Download **here** and on my website
**https://alchemytherapies.co.uk**

# REFERENCES

[1] Pesonen. A (2005), Continuity of maternal stress from the pre- to the postnatal period: associations with infant's positive, negative and overall temperamental reactivity, Infant Behavior Development,28, 1,p36-47, https://doi.org/10.1016/j.infbeh.2004.09.001.

[2] Aron, E.N. and A. Aron, Sensory-processing sensitivity and its relation to introversion and emotionality. *J Pers Soc Psychol,* 1997. 73(2): p. 345-68.

[3] May, A. et al. Early predictors of sensory processing sensitivity in members of the Birth to Twenty Plus cohort, *J. Res. Personality,* 2023. 104 p370, https://doi.org/10.1016/j.jrp.2023.104370.

[4] Meaney, M, Szyf, M. & Seckl, J. (2007). Epigenetic mechanisms of perinatal programming of hypothalamic-pituitary-adrenal function and health. *Trends Mol Med.* 13. 269-77. 10.1016/j.molmed.2007.05.003.

[5] Barker DJ. In utero programming of chronic disease. Clin Sci (Lond). 1998 Aug;95(2):115-28. PMID: 9680492.

[6] Barker DJ. The developmental origins of well-being. *Philos Trans R Soc Lond B Biol Sci.* 2004 Sep 29;359(1449):1359-66. doi: 10.1098/rstb.2004.1518

[7] Boyce, W. et al. (1995). Psychobiologic Reactivity to Stress and Childhood Respiratory Illnesses: Results of Two Prospective Studies. *Psychosomatic medicine.* 57. 411-22. 10.1097/00006842-199509000-00001.

[8] Lionetti, et al. (2018). Dandelions, tulips and orchids: Evidence for the existence of low-sensitive, medium-sensitive and high-sensitive individuals. Translational Psychiatry. 8. 10.1038/s41398-017-0090-6.

# ABOUT THE AUTHOR

Patricia Worby, PhD, MSc, BSc is a former scientist, now a researcher and specialist practitioner in chronic fatigue and pain. She worked for the NHS and then the University of Southampton in clinical research and latterly as a Research Manager - for a total of 25 years. After graduation she was going to 'change the world through science' but life intervened in a quite unexpected way.

After a series of health challenges in her 30's, including depression and chronic fatigue, she was encouraged to find her own answers and is now a passionate advocate of natural medicine. Today, she is a holistic therapist who specialises in chronic illness, especially ME/CFS and Fibromyalgia using nutrition, massage and emotional healing. She completed her PhD on the links between implicit memory and chronic pain in 2016 and since then has developed numerous courses to help people heal including the Emotional AUDIT programme (self-study or group course) and works 121 with people from across the world.

She can be found online at **www.alchemytherapies.co.uk** (therapy) and **www.patriciaworby.co.uk** (education/science)

Printed in Great Britain
by Amazon

28275301R00110